ULTIMATE CHRISTMAS

ULTIMATE CHRISTMAS

The Essential Recipes & Festive
Crafts for the Perfect Christmas

Love Food ® is an imprint of Parragon Books Ltd
This edition published in 2008 for Index Books Ltd

Parragon
Queen Street House
4 Queen Street
Bath BA1 1HE, UK

ISBN: 978-1-4075-0339-4
Printed in China

Cover by Talking Design
Produced by the Bridgewater Book Company Ltd
Craft projects created and written by Emma Frith
New recipes written by Sarah Banbery
Introduction written by Sara Harper
Craft projects photography by Andrew Perris
Craft projects styled by Isabel de Cordova
New recipe photography by Laurie Evans
Home economy by Carol Tennant
Additional photography by Mark Wood

The publisher would like to thank the following for permission to reproduce copyright material: Bettmann/Corbis: 4; Dorling Kindersley/Getty Images: 10 (top); Photonica/Getty Images: 10 (bottom); Mike Bentley/iStockphoto: 11; Sergej Petrakov/iStockphoto: 12; Lisa Thornberg/iStockphoto: 13; The Image Bank/Getty Images: 14; Iconica/Getty Images: 16; Jupiter Images: 17; StockFood/Getty Images: 21; and Malte Danielsson/Etsa/Corbis: 25.

Notes for the Reader

This book uses both metric and imperial measurements. Follow the same units of measurement throughout; do not mix metric and imperial. All spoon measurements are level: teaspoons are assumed to be 5 ml, and tablespoons are assumed to be 15 ml. Unless otherwise stated, milk is assumed to be full fat, eggs and individual vegetables such as potatoes are medium and pepper is freshly ground black pepper. Recipes using raw or very lightly cooked eggs should be avoided by infants, the elderly, pregnant women, convalescents and anyone suffering from an illness. The times given are an approximate guide only.

Contents

Introduction

Christmas is the time to make your home warm and welcoming, festoon it with festive decorations and infuse it with the aroma of enticing foods made from favourite recipes handed down over the years. It's a time of goodwill and giving, for celebrating with family and close friends. For many people, the religious aspect of Christmas has all but disappeared, but there's still a good underlying reason to celebrate. It's not about spending vast amounts of money in an effort to outdo and impress; it's about having a good time with people you care about. This is the perfect guide for creating a memorable Christmas at home, with fresh and inspiring ideas for making the most of the festive season.

In this book, you'll find out why we celebrate Christmas and where most of our traditions come from. There are even suggestions to help you establish your own customs,

to make Christmas even more special for you. To reduce the stress of the Christmas season, there's a section on getting organized, with a Christmas diary, handy tips on choosing a good Christmas tree and suggestions for organizing a party and how to entertain your guests.

You will also find a selection of craft projects for you and your family to undertake, including ideas for making beautiful cards and simple decorations for your home.

COOKING AT CHRISTMAS

Whether your Christmas dinner is a huge family feast or a quiet dinner for one or two, you'll find plenty of recipe ideas to suit every occasion. This book features a tempting blend of favourite traditional recipes and updated classics with a contemporary twist, so you can keep up with family traditions and create some new ones of your own. Easy yet impressive recipes will inspire you to make fabulous food for friends

and family throughout the festive season, with irresistible options to satisfy meat-eaters and vegetarians alike. There's advice on planning your Christmas feast and suggestions for managing your Christmas cooking, enabling you to get the preparations under control and giving you the chance to relax and enjoy the day with your friends and family. Finally, there are helpful tips on turkeys and also ideas for decorating your table.

You don't need a mind-boggling array of kitchen equipment, nor do you need to be a culinary genius to create these mouthwatering meals. The recipes are clear and easy to follow, with gorgeous full-colour photography throughout to enable you to produce fabulous food effortlessly, every time. The recipes have been devised with an underlying understanding of which ingredients work together in the pan and on the plate for spectacular results, and the ingredients are seasonal and readily sourced.

CHAPTER 1

All About
Chris

tmas

Christmas is an important occasion in the
year because it's a time when we get together with family
and friends. The following pages explain why we celebrate
Christmas, and give an insight into the many traditions
that have arisen over the years. There is also a practical
guide on how to organize and prepare for the festive
season well in advance.

What is *Christmas?*

Christmas is a celebration of the birth of Christ, although no-one knows the day when he was actually born. Today, it's a major holiday and holy day, and even those who are not religious observe this festival as a special time to spend with families and friends.

The practice of celebrating the 25th day of December as Christ's birthday originates from the 4th century (before this time it had been a movable feast), and the choice of this particular day was probably influenced by pagan festivals held at that time. During the 6th century, the tradition of the twelve-day holy festival was established, starting on Christmas Day and ending on the morning of the Epiphany (6 January). The Epiphany either marks the arrival of the three wise men or the magi bearing gifts, or Christ's baptism, depending on which particular type of Christianity people follow.

The popularity of Christmas grew until the Reformation, a time of widespread religious upheaval that caused many Christians to stop celebrating Christmas because it included so many pagan customs. In many countries, Christmas festivities didn't become that important again until the 19th century, when Charles Dickens wrote *A Christmas Carol* and St Nicholas was transformed into Father Christmas, changing the spirit of Christmas into what we recognize today. Dickens's book had an extremely powerful influence on undermining opposition to Christmas. Dickens used Scrooge to symbolize the idea that those who don't celebrate Christmas are uncharitable and mean-spirited. And central to the Dickens Christmas celebration was a lavish family dinner.

HOW CHRISTMAS IS CELEBRATED TODAY

The celebration of Christmas is the most popular religious-based public festival in the world and its arrival in December is often prepared for months in advance by some people. During the Christmas season, people decorate their homes, city streets sparkle with coloured lights, and the sound of Christmas music, both traditional carols and more modern popular songs, fills the air. Many department stores hire people to dress up as Father Christmas and listen to children's requests for gifts. People share festive greetings by sending Christmas cards to relatives and friends. On Christmas Eve, children hang up stockings for Father Christmas to fill with gifts, and many people go to a carol concert in church. Christmas Day usually culminates in the unwrapping of presents and a fabulous feast.

How to survive & enjoy the Christmas season

There's a saying that at Christmas-time it's a race to see which will give out first – your feet or your wallet. To make your Christmas more pleasurable, follow these top tips:

* Try to avoid being too ambitious when you are choosing presents (this will help your bank balance as well).
* Many shops allow you to order online, minimizing time spent in crowded shops.
* Scale down your ambitions. If you're a working parent, you'll wear yourself ragged if you feel obliged to do everything yourself, from baking to card making. Choose one thing that you really enjoy doing (such as making biscuits with your children) to make Christmas special and save the rest for years when you're not so short of time.
* Establish your own traditions instead of doing what everyone else does.
* Avoid family conflicts and call a truce on unresolved problems.
* Share the workload – invite your guests to bring canapés or puddings to your party instead of trying to do all the cooking and baking yourself.
* Give yourself a break. Although finding time for yourself may seem almost impossible at this time of year, if you do, you're more likely to relax. And if you're relaxed, your family and friends are more likely to enjoy themselves.

Christmas
Traditions

There are numerous traditions that are associated with Christmas, from giving gifts and cards to one another and decorating a tree, to hanging a wreath on the door and kissing under the mistletoe, but do you know where some of these traditions originated from?

The Christmas season is steeped in familiar, old traditions. Decorating our homes, trimming the tree and exchanging gifts are staples of the season. When you take into account the bleakness of winter, it's no surprise that throughout history people have celebrated the winter solstice (the shortest day of the year), which heralds the arrival of longer days and the renewal of spring. Countless traditions are associated with midwinter celebrations. Here, you'll find a brief explanation of why we celebrate in some of the ways that we do.

PRESENTS

The tradition of gifts seems to have started with those that the wise men (the magi) brought to Jesus. Gift-giving at Christmas was rare in Europe or America before the 19th century, but the Santa Claus story, combined with an amazing retailing phenomenon that has grown over the past 100 years or so, has made giving gifts the central focus of the Christmas tradition. In the 19th century, gifts tended to be made by the giver and were practical, such as gloves or food, but modern gifts tend to be more frivolous, fun or luxurious.

CHRISTMAS CARDS

Christmas cards were introduced in 1843 by Sir Henry Cole, an English businessman and patron of art, who printed 1,000 cards and sold them as a means to simplify the sending of Christmas greetings. Nowadays, because we are all so busy, it's much more common for us to keep in touch with family and friends simply by mailing a card or even emailing greetings rather than buying a gift and giving it to them in person.

THE CHRISTMAS TREE

Ancient Egyptians used palms in their winter solstice festivals, and the Romans used firs, in anticipation of the lush greenery of spring with the return of the sun. Bringing an evergreen tree into the house was a long-standing German tradition, made popular in the UK after the German Prince Albert married Queen Victoria. The Germans also decorated their trees with tinsel, fruits, pastries, sweets, coloured paper figures, tin angels and other ornaments. Today, some form of Christmas tree, replete with all kinds of decorations, forms part of every Christmas celebration. And if you mount a star on top, it represents the star that led the wise men to the stable in Bethlehem.

Candles were traditionally placed in windows to help travellers to find and identify houses, and to create festive cheer. Decorating houses, trees and gardens with strings of multicoloured lights for the Christmas period became popular in the 20th century.

CHRISTMAS WREATHS

In ancient Rome, people used decorative wreaths as a sign of victory and celebration, and the custom of hanging a Christmas wreath on the front door of the home probably started then. Today, there are two types of Christmas wreath: one that is made for decoration, and the other an advent wreath that has four coloured candles lit on consecutive Sundays as a religious countdown to Christmas. The Christmas wreath symbolizes the strength of life overcoming the forces of winter. It is formed in a circle to signify eternity and usually hung on the front door to encourage happiness and good fortune in the New Year.

MISTLETOE AND HOLLY

These plants have long been associated with Christmas, and used in all types of decoration. Mistletoe is a symbol of peace and joy, and in ancient Britain, the Druids regarded it as sacred. Native Americans also regarded mistletoe as sacred, while the Scandinavians associated it with the goddess of love. The unholy and pagan associations with mistletoe (not forgetting the kissing, which is regarded as a sign of friendship and goodwill) caused the church to ban its use and substitute holly instead, whose needle-like leaf points represented the crown of thorns Jesus wore when crucified; the red berries symbolized the drops of blood that He shed.

COLOURS OF CHRISTMAS

The traditional colours of Christmas are green and red. Green represents the continuance of life through the winter and the Christian belief in eternal life through Christ. Red symbolizes the blood that Christians believe Jesus shed at his crucifixion.

ST NICHOLAS AND SANTA CLAUS

The transformation of St Nicholas to Santa Claus (or Father Christmas) happened largely in America. St Nicholas was a 4th-century Turkish bishop, whose reputation for generosity and kindness gave rise to all kinds of legends about miracles he performed. After the Reformation, Nicholas's cult disappeared in all the Protestant countries of Europe except Holland, where his legend persisted as Sinterklaas (a Dutch variant of the name St Nicholas). Dutch colonists took this tradition with them to the American colonies in the 17th century.

But the popular view of Santa that we all have today, along with the customary sleigh, the reindeer and the chimney, dates from the 19th century, when the poem 'The Night Before Christmas' names the reindeer, invents the sleigh and sends St Nick down the chimney. Also, a series of engravings run by a popular magazine of the time depicted a jolly Santa in his workshop, reading letters, checking his list and so on. But the red and white suit did come from the original St Nicholas – those being the colours of a bishop's robes.

CHRISTMAS STOCKINGS

If you hang a stocking at the end of your bed or on your mantelpiece, it's because of St Nicholas. According to legend, he took pity on a poverty-stricken family with three daughters, who had no wedding dowries. For two of the daughters, he crept up to their house at night and threw bags of gold through a window. For the last daughter, he threw a bag of gold down the chimney, which landed in a stocking she had set by the fireplace for drying.

RUDOLPH THE RED-NOSED REINDEER

The story of Rudolph, whose glowing nose is used as a navigational device, was created in 1939 by Robert May for a Chicago department store as a promotional gimmick. Johnny Marks, May's brother-in-law, eventually developed May's original story into lyrics and melody for a song, and Gene Autry's 1949 recording of it sold over 2 million copies, making it one of the best-selling Christmas records of all time.

CHRISTMAS MUSIC

Originally, carols were songs for celebration, and today they can include both religious songs, such as 'Silent Night', as well as non-religious songs like 'Jingle Bells'. Christmas music now includes classical pieces, popular tunes and rock music. Bells are rung to announce the birth of Jesus, but may date back to pagan methods of warding off evil spirits.

ADVENT CALENDARS

Advent remains a season of spiritual preparation, and in many countries people use special calendars to count down to Christmas. A traditional advent calendar consists of two pieces of cardboard placed on top of each other. Twenty-four doors are cut out in the top layer, with one door being opened every day from 1 December until Christmas Eve to reveal a picture or a sweet behind each compartment.

A Partridge in a Pear Tree

The carol 'The Twelve Days of Christmas' was supposedly created to keep the Catholic faith alive during a time of religious persecution – for example, the partridge was Jesus and the ten lords were the ten commandments. But it's more likely that it was just sung as an aid to help young children learn to count.

CREATING YOUR OWN TRADITIONS

If kissing under the mistletoe or singing carols around the Christmas tree just isn't your idea of fun, why not create some new customs for you to enjoy? You can make this season extra special if you take the time to create your own unique customs for you and your household.

The best way to do this is to hold a household meeting and get everyone to make a suggestion, then you can debate the merits of each. Possible options include:

* A special book to read.
* A family outing.
* A classic film to watch.
* Making some edible treats together.
* A countryside walk through the woods in search of reindeer on Christmas Eve.
* Taking a photo of your children every year: date and frame them, then hang them on the tree, so that as they grow up, the children can see how much they've changed.

Countdown to *Christmas*

This section deals with the practical aspects of Christmas, from how to organize your time, to shopping wisely and choosing a tree. You'll also find a Christmas planning diary as well as useful advice for organizing a party.

ORGANIZING YOUR TIME

You don't need to start thinking about Christmas in July, but if you can start planning a few weeks ahead, it does make things easier. Find a calendar, notebook and pen to plan out the festive season, then make a note of all the important dates such as school plays, concerts, church services, theatre trips and visits to relatives.

Get a folder for storing magazine articles, recipes and any relevant notes – you can add to this each year with all sorts of ideas for gifts, parties, activities and menus.

HOW TO AVOID CREDIT CARD DEBT

It's all too easy to get caught up in a frenzy of Christmas shopping and spend up to the limit on your credit cards, but with a little forethought you needn't end up in debt.

- Spread your Christmas spending throughout the year if you love to lavish family members with expensive gifts during the festive season and you don't want to stop the practice.

- Set aside a fixed amount each month to cover Christmas expenditure.

- Set a Christmas budget. Decide what you can reasonably afford to spend and do not go above that amount, even if it means sacrificing gifts along the way.

- Buy only for those closest to you.

- Shop around to find bargains and discounts and possibly wait for last-minute reductions, or think ahead and store away items purchased in the January sales.

- Save money and have fun at the same time by handcrafting some presents or baking some edible gifts using the ideas in this book.

HOW TO CHOOSE A CHRISTMAS TREE

A favourite Christmas tradition is choosing and decorating your Christmas tree, and the main options are pre-cut (convenient but costly) or cut-your-own (effort required). The major drawback to both pre-cut and cut-your-own trees is that they are dead, so they will dry out and drop needles all over your floor and your gifts. And the drier they get, the more of a fire hazard they are. A potted tree is the freshest option, but then there's the problem of where to put it afterwards. Or you could opt for an artificial tree – there are no worries over disposal, the needles won't drop off and create a mess, it's easy to store away and you can use it again year after year.

* Know how tall your ceiling is and how much floor space you have available.
* If it will be on view from all sides, you'll want a symmetrical tree. If the tree will be going up against a wall, it doesn't matter if one side is less than perfect.
* Remember to take a tape measure with you to measure the tree.
* Look for a tree with a straight base, about 15-20 cm/6-8 inches long, so that you can make a fresh cut and still have room to fit it into your stand.
* Bear in mind the sturdiness of the branches. Many pines make tempting choices because of their long needles, but the branches will bend under the weight of even small ornaments.
* A fresh tree will look healthy and green, with few browning needles. The needles will feel pliable, and when broken and squeezed, they will exude pitch. To test whether a tree is fresh, carefully rub your hand along a branch to see if any needles fall off.

LOOKING AFTER YOUR TREE

The most important thing you can do is keep the tree watered. Make a fresh cut at the bottom of the tree at least 2.5 cm/1 inch above the original cut, then fill the reservoir with lukewarm water. Check and fill the reservoir often – Christmas trees become a fire hazard when their moisture content falls below 50 per cent.

SAFETY TIPS

* Keep the tree away from open flames and other sources of heat. Even some appliances, like your TV, can heat up sufficiently to be hazardous.
* Keep tinsel away from light sockets.
* Always check your lights before you put them on the tree. Replace tree lights that have loose connections or exposed, brittle or cracked wires, and never leave the lights on unattended.
* Don't leave light wires trailing along the floor for people to trip over.

Christmas Planner
Diary

During the festive season there is plenty to organize and prepare, so it's a good idea to plan well in advance and then you will be ready for the big day when it arrives.

Checklist

WEEK 1 (END NOVEMBER/BEGINNING DECEMBER)
* Set your budget.
* Write your card list.
* Write your gift list and start buying presents.
* Pack up and send overseas cards and presents.
* Plan parties and activities for the season.

WEEK 2
* Presents – buy the biggest ones first so that you don't overspend on buying small gifts for others.
* Make your own Christmas cards and decorations if time allows.
* Get the Christmas decorations out of the attic, and test and replace Christmas lights if necessary.

WEEK 3
* Send off Christmas cards before the final post day.
* Finalize your Christmas menu.
* Buy plenty of wrapping paper and tape, and start wrapping presents.

* Start a detailed grocery shopping list – put it up on the refrigerator and add to it as you think of items.
* Get the tree and decorate it – you could even hold a decorating party.

CHRISTMAS WEEK
* Tidy up your house and make sure the areas that are going to be in frequent use by guests (such as bathrooms) are sparkling clean.
* Hang up Christmas decorations.
* Put the presents under the tree.
* Do the big Christmas food shop.

CHRISTMAS EVE
* Peel and cut all vegetables, and store in sealed containers in the refrigerator. Prepare and chill desserts, defrost the turkey, make seasoning mixes and make or start accompanying sauces.
* Hang up the Christmas stockings and look forward to the big day tomorrow.

PARTY PLANNING

Whether it's a small gathering or a cast of hundreds, hosting a party is a great way to celebrate the festive season with friends and family. You don't need a degree in party planning to host a Christmas bash, but you need more than a few cheap crackers and cooking sherry to make your guests rave about your merrymaking for months to come. Organization and careful planning are key to a great get-together. Organize everything in advance and create a detailed checklist, timetable and to-do list. Constantly update your lists and keep all the papers together for quick reference. They can also form the basis for future party plans.

Set the budget. You need to know from the start how much you want to spend so that you don't have to cut back later. If you can afford only so much food or drink, then invite fewer guests rather than scrimping and saving – or, if you know your guests very well, ask them to contribute.

Food needs to look gorgeous, be appetizing and taste delicious. Make sure you have plenty of options for vegetarians and guests on special or religious diets. Party food needs to be eaten easily with one hand, because your guests are bound to have a glass in the other, so keep the food very simple and preferably bite-sized.

Don't rule out convenience foods and don't feel that everything has to be home-made – supplement a party buffet with a few shop-bought crudités and dips, with plenty of fresh crusty bread and a selection of cheeses in reserve. The idea is to minimize your efforts so that you haven't exhausted yourself before the party even begins.

Serve glasses of hot mulled wine for a festive feel and don't forget to offer plenty of non-alcoholic options such as fresh fruit juices, fizzy drinks, cordials and sparkling water. Try to keep your selection of drinks simple, and allow at least two glasses per person.

Finally, get yourself ready in plenty of time and be a guest at your own party rather than hiding in the kitchen. Smile and look as though you are enjoying yourself, and then everyone else will, too.

If you've got friends or family staying over, you'll probably feel the need to lay on a little festive entertainment. This doesn't have to be very elaborate or even obligatory, and need involve no more than a few board games, console or video games or clearing a space for dancing. Try to set aside a suitable space in your home, such as the living room or conservatory, with perhaps a few bowls of nibbles to hand and a selection of soft drinks in the vicinity for people to help themselves to. If the weather is good, then outside activities could be as simple as a treasure hunt around the garden or even in the countryside.

Christmas
Reci

*T*he excitement of preparations, the activity, the music, the lights and the tantalizing aromas that pervade the home at this time of year all add to the magic of Christmas. Whether you are planning a small family get-together, a party for friends or a much larger celebration, then the following pages will help you plan and create the perfect Christmas feast.

pes

The Christmas
Feast

The feast is the focal point of the celebrations. Although to some extent food is a significant part of all holidays, it doesn't pack the same symbolic punch as that of a Christmas feast.

Christmas is traditionally a time of indulgence and good food, a time to ditch the diet and spoil yourself a little. December feasts have always been common in the northern hemisphere, even in pagan times, because in the old days it was necessary to slaughter cattle that would otherwise have been too expensive

to feed during the winter, and because the meat could be preserved by the cold weather. With the completion of the harvest and with snow on the ground, farmers were loaded with provisions. There was not much work that could be done, so it was an opportunity to relax, to feast, to celebrate and to engage in social activities before the hard, lean months of winter set in.

The food that's traditionally on offer during the Christmas period reflects a particular country's climate and what's always been seasonally available, from dried fruits and nuts to root vegetables and fattened poultry, game and meat. It's high-calorie food, too, because during the cold weather we need more calories just to stay warm, although that's not always the case in these days of central heating, so remember this when you reach for a third mince pie!

There's a scrumptious array of mouthwatering food that's customarily eaten at Christmas, packed with robust flavours and enticing aromas. Food fashions come and go, but anyone planning a Christmas feast today would normally choose from starters such as prawn cocktail, chicken liver

pâté or smoked salmon with cream cheese. The centrepiece of the Christmas feast is usually a succulent turkey with cranberry sauce and a host of enticing seasonal vegetables on the side. Trimmings include Brussels sprouts with buttered chestnuts, glazed parsnips, cranberry sauce and chestnut and sausage stuffing. Although turkey is the usual choice nowadays for Christmas lunch, there are numerous other traditional meat treats that you can enjoy, including game, goose and duck, which are all at their best during Christmas. Glazed gammon and poached salmon are also festive favourites, as is nut roast for vegetarians.

Desserts that are traditionally eaten during the festive period tend to be dense and calorie-laden, and include brandy snaps, Christmas pudding and trifle. And your waistband might expand even more with mince pies, Christmas cake, chocolate yule log, truffles and lashings of brandy butter, to say nothing of a host of hearty alcoholic beverages, such as mulled wine or mulled ale, designed to warm you up and get you into the spirit of the season.

TOP TIPS WHEN PLANNING A CHRISTMAS FEAST

Planning a Christmas dinner isn't complicated, but the more forethought you give it, the easier it will be. The key is to do as much ahead of time as you can, to allow you to enjoy the big day.

- Decide how many guests you'll have, and work out how much space is available, both at the table and in your home.
- Draw up your menu and choose dishes that are both delicious and easy to make. Choose recipes that can be made ahead of time or that require just a little heating right before the feast to be completed. Another thing to remember when planning your menu is never choose a recipe that you have not tried before. Select reliable favourites, or, if you would like to add a new dish to your traditional menu, practise making it beforehand.
- Organize the menu into to-do lists, including all preparation steps.
- Empty as much of the refrigerator as possible.
- Make the big trip to the supermarket a few days in advance. Most items, with the exception of fruit and vegetables, will keep for a week.
- Set the table and get your home ready two days ahead, if seating people at a table for dinner. This will give you enough time to buy or borrow things you may need.
- Buffet service is easier to manage than seating everyone at the same table. Set the table against a wall and use it as the serving area. For a buffet, divide all the food into small portions.
- Plan your guests' arrival to give you enough time to cook.
- Serve some food that doesn't need to be cooked, like salad, cheese and fresh fruit.

CAN YOUR KITCHEN COPE?

It's pointless to plan a feast that your kitchen can't handle. Every kitchen has space limitations; make sure you know yours. For example, is your cooker big enough to heat the five dishes you plan to serve hot at the same time? And how large is your refrigerator? Large enough to fit in all those platters of cold canapés? If not, now's the time to make adjustments and substitutions.

AVOID KITCHEN CHAOS Choose an array of foods served at a variety of temperatures and prepare as many dishes in advance as possible. Don't forget to allow enough time for defrosting and reheating your food on the day of the party.

Remember that food takes longer to cook when there are several dishes in the oven at the same time, so it's better to cook some food ahead and keep it warm rather than finding something is undercooked when you're ready to serve.

Line roasting trays with foil and discard at the end of cooking to make washing up easier, and wash up as you go along to avoid accumulating a mountain of pots, pans and kitchen clutter.

MAKE AS MUCH AHEAD AS YOU CAN Waiting until the last few days before your feast to cook everything just doesn't make sense, especially when, if you examine your menu, you'll see that much of it can be prepared ahead, frozen and reheated. Just pin up a reminder to yourself so you don't forget to defrost in time.

Christmas cake and pudding can be made months ahead and are all the better for it, so set aside an afternoon for baking and roll up your sleeves. Biscuit dough can be frozen for several weeks before you need it, as can mince pies. If

you're serving a decorated cake, make and bake the cake parts a week or more ahead of time, wrap them well in clingfilm and freeze them until the day before. Frozen cakes are easier to decorate than thawed ones anyway.

STORING FOOD If you run out of space, be creative. You can store food temporarily in the microwave or on top of the washing machine. If it's really cold outside, a garden shed or garage can serve as a second refrigerator.

TALKING TURKEY

If you know the size of bird you'll need and how to cook it, you're halfway to creating a successful Christmas dinner.

The amount of people you can feed with a particular bird will depend on how meaty it is, but as a rule of thumb a small turkey or goose will serve 4–7 people, a medium one 8–11, a large one 12–15 and an extra-large turkey (over 8 kg/17 lb 10 oz) will serve up to 20.

For frozen birds, defrost in the fridge, allowing 18 hours per 1 kg/2 lb 4 oz, or in a cool place for 7 hours per 1 kg/2 lb 4 oz.

Cook the turkey up to an hour in advance and keep it warm by wrapping it in a double layer of foil then cover it with a tea towel while other dishes are cooking to avoid last-minute panic.

Let the meat rest for at least 30 minutes before carving – this lets the juices settle back into the meat, making it more succulent and easier to carve.

DECORATING YOUR TABLE

A beautifully set table can make even plain food look elegant and inviting, and you don't need to spend a lot of money to do it. Start with a

tablecloth, especially if your dining-room table has seen better days. Tablecloths cover a multitude of sins while adding colour and pattern. If you don't own the perfect tablecloth, rummage through charity and junk shops for old linens or even a beautiful sheet. Use prints sparingly, though, to avoid the table looking too busy. Squares of silk can make a dramatic statement when artfully draped over a plain white tablecloth.

When it comes to centrepieces, don't limit your thinking to flowers, wreaths or pine cones sprayed with gold and silver paint (although these are all attractive and festive decorations). A bowl of colourful fruits or vegetables such as kumquats or chilli peppers, Christmas baubles, or even small bright toys can add charm and character to your table setting, depending on how you arrange them. If you are using foliage or fresh flowers, make sure it is clean before placing it near any food.

As for the rest of the table, it's up to you which china, glasswear and cutlery you use (matching if possible), whether to have festive napkin rings and placemats, or a selection of Christmas crackers or small gifts for your guests.

You just can't go wrong with candles. Candlelight is warm, cosy and very festive. Avoid using scented candles because their fragrance may compete with the aromas of your Christmas cooking. Otherwise, candles of various heights look especially lovely when grouped together on mirrored surfaces (you could use a small wall mirror with the hanger on the back removed, or even a mirrored tile), and can form a backdrop to any number of different centrepieces. You can use either simple white candles in plain holders or candles in the traditional festive colours of red and green to add further colour to your table.

Starters, Brunches

& Lunches

Wild Mushroom &

Sherry Soup

SERVES 4

2 tbsp olive oil
1 onion, chopped
1 garlic clove, chopped
125 g/4½ oz sweet potato,
   peeled and chopped
1 leek, trimmed and sliced
200 g/7 oz button and
   chestnut mushrooms
150 g/5½ oz mixed
   wild mushrooms
600 ml/1 pint vegetable stock
350 ml/12 fl oz single cream
4 tbsp dry sherry
salt and pepper

TO GARNISH
Parmesan cheese shavings
sautéed wild mushrooms, sliced

★ Heat the oil in a saucepan over a medium heat. Add the onion and garlic and cook, stirring, for 3 minutes, until slightly softened. Add the sweet potato and cook, stirring, for 3 minutes. Add the leek and cook, stirring, for 2 minutes.

★ Stir in the mushrooms, stock and cream. Bring to the boil, then reduce the heat and simmer gently, stirring occasionally, for 25 minutes. Remove from the heat, stir in the sherry and leave to cool slightly.

★ Transfer half the soup to a food processor and blend until smooth. Return the mixture to the saucepan with the rest of the soup, season to taste with salt and pepper and reheat gently, stirring. Pour into 4 warmed soup bowls and garnish with Parmesan cheese shavings and sautéed wild mushrooms.

COOK'S NOTE

★ An increasing range of wild mushrooms is now available in supermarkets. If fresh ones are not available, use 40-55 g/1½-2 oz dried instead. Soak them in hot water for 30 minutes and drain well before using.

Spiced Pumpkin

Soup

SERVES 4

2 tbsp olive oil
1 onion, chopped
1 garlic clove, chopped
1 tbsp chopped fresh root ginger
1 small red chilli, deseeded and
    finely chopped
2 tbsp chopped fresh coriander
1 bay leaf
1 kg/2 lb 4 oz pumpkin, peeled,
    deseeded and diced
600 ml/1 pint vegetable stock
salt and pepper
single cream, to garnish

✦ Heat the oil in a saucepan over a medium heat. Add the onion and garlic and cook, stirring, for 4 minutes, until slightly softened. Add the ginger, chilli, coriander, bay leaf and pumpkin and cook, stirring, for 3 minutes.

✦ Pour in the stock and bring to the boil. Using a slotted spoon, skim any scum from the surface. Reduce the heat and simmer gently, stirring occasionally, for 25 minutes, or until the pumpkin is tender. Remove from the heat, take out and discard the bay leaf and leave to cool slightly.

✦ Transfer the soup to a food processor and blend until smooth (you may have to do this in batches). Return the mixture to the saucepan and season to taste with salt and pepper. Reheat gently, stirring. Remove from the heat, pour into 4 warmed soup bowls, garnish each one with a swirl of cream and serve.

COOK'S NOTE

✦ Even so-called pie pumpkins are often larger than required, so you may need to buy a section of a larger one to avoid waste (they are often sold by the piece). Check that the flesh is firm and has not dried out and become unpleasantly fibrous.

Mozzarella Crostini
with Pesto & Caviar

SERVES 4

8 slices white bread,
   crusts removed
3 tbsp olive oil
200 g/7 oz firm mozzarella
   cheese, diced
6 tbsp lumpfish roe

PESTO
75 g/2¾ oz fresh basil,
   finely chopped
35 g/1¼ oz pine kernels,
   finely chopped
2 garlic cloves, finely chopped
3 tbsp olive oil

★ Preheat the oven to 180°C/350°F/Gas Mark 4. Using a sharp knife, cut the bread into fancy shapes, such as half-moons, stars and Christmas trees. Drizzle with the oil, transfer to an ovenproof dish and bake in the preheated oven for 15 minutes.

★ While the bread is baking, make the pesto. Put the basil, pine kernels and garlic in a small bowl. Pour in the oil and stir well.

★ Remove the bread shapes from the oven and leave to cool. Spread a layer of pesto on the shapes, top each one with a piece of mozzarella and some lumpfish roe and serve.

COOK'S NOTE

★ Lumpfish roe is often coloured black to resemble caviar, although it may also be dyed orange or red. The colour tends to run, so do not top the crostini until you are ready to serve. You could use naturally coloured roes, such as keta salmon roe or trout roe, which do not run.

Chicken Liver
Pâté

SERVES 4–6

200 g/7 oz butter
225 g/8 oz trimmed chicken
   livers, thawed if frozen
2 tbsp Marsala wine or brandy
1½ tsp chopped fresh sage
1 garlic clove, roughly chopped
150 ml/5 fl oz double cream
salt and pepper
fresh bay leaves or sage leaves,
   to garnish
Melba toast (see Cook's Note,
   below), to serve

★ Melt 40 g/1½ oz of the butter in a large, heavy-based frying pan. Add the chicken livers and cook over a medium heat for 4 minutes on each side. They should be browned on the outside but still pink in the centre. Transfer to a food processor and process until finely chopped.

★ Stir the Marsala into the frying pan, scraping up any sediment with a wooden spoon, then add to the food processor with the chopped sage, garlic and 100 g/3½ oz of the remaining butter. Process until smooth. Add the cream, season to taste with salt and pepper and process until thoroughly combined and smooth. Spoon the pâté into a dish or individual ramekins, smooth the surface and leave to cool completely.

★ Melt the remaining butter in a small saucepan, then spoon it over the surface of the pâté, leaving any sediment in the saucepan. Decorate with herb leaves, leave to cool, then cover and chill in the refrigerator. Serve with Melba toast.

COOK'S NOTE

★ To make Melba toast, grill slices of white bread on both sides until golden. Cut off and discard the crusts and slice the bread in half horizontally. Grill the cut sides until golden and the edges are curling. Cool and store in an airtight container until required.

Festive Prawn
Cocktail

SERVES 8

125 ml/4 fl oz tomato ketchup
1 tsp chilli sauce
1 tsp Worcestershire sauce
1 kg/2 lb 4 oz cooked tiger prawns
2 ruby grapefruits
lettuce leaves, shredded
2 avocados, peeled, stoned
   and diced

MAYONNAISE
2 large egg yolks
1 tsp English mustard powder
1 tsp salt
300 ml/10 fl oz groundnut oil
1 tsp white wine vinegar
pepper

TO GARNISH
lime slices
fresh dill sprigs

✦ First make the mayonnaise. Put the egg yolks in a bowl, add the mustard powder, pepper to taste and salt and beat together well. Pour the oil into a jug and make sure that your bowl is secure on the work surface by sitting it on a damp cloth. Using an electric or hand whisk, begin to whisk the egg yolks, adding just 1 drop of the oil. Make sure that this has been thoroughly absorbed before adding another drop and whisking well.

✦ Continue adding the oil 1 drop at a time until the mixture thickens and stiffens - at this point, whisk in the vinegar and then continue to dribble in the remaining oil very slowly in a thin stream, whisking constantly, until you have used up all the oil and you have a thick mayonnaise.

✦ Mix the mayonnaise, tomato ketchup, chilli sauce and Worcestershire sauce together in a small bowl. Cover with clingfilm and refrigerate until required.

✦ Remove the heads from the prawns and peel off the shells, leaving the tails intact. Slit along the length of the back of each prawn with a sharp knife and remove and discard the dark vein. Cut off a slice from the top and bottom of each grapefruit, then peel off the skin and all the white pith. Cut between the membranes to separate the segments.

✦ When ready to serve, make a bed of shredded lettuce in the base of 8 glass dishes. Divide the prawns, grapefruit segments and avocados between them and spoon over the mayonnaise dressing. Serve the cocktails garnished with lime slices and dill sprigs.

Turkey Club
Sandwiches

SERVES 6

SANDWICHES
12 pancetta or streaky
    bacon rashers
18 slices white bread
12 slices cooked turkey
    breast meat
3 plum tomatoes, sliced
6 Little Gem lettuce leaves
6 stuffed olives
salt and pepper

MAYONNAISE
2 large egg yolks
1 tsp English mustard powder
1 tsp salt
300 ml/10 fl oz groundnut oil
1 tsp white wine vinegar
pepper

★ First make the mayonnaise. Put the egg yolks in a bowl, add the mustard powder, pepper to taste and salt and beat together well. Pour the oil into a jug and make sure that your bowl is secure on the work surface by sitting it on a damp cloth. Using an electric or hand whisk, begin to whisk the egg yolks, adding just 1 drop of the oil. Make sure that this has been thoroughly absorbed before adding another drop and whisking well.

★ Continue adding the oil 1 drop at a time until the mixture thickens and stiffens - at this point, whisk in the vinegar and then continue to dribble in the remaining oil very slowly in a thin stream, whisking constantly, until you have used up all the oil and you have a thick mayonnaise. Cover and refrigerate while you prepare the other sandwich components.

★ Grill or fry the pancetta until crisp, drain on kitchen paper and keep warm. Toast the bread until golden, then cut off the crusts.

★ You will need 3 slices of toast for each sandwich. For each sandwich, spread the first piece of toast with a generous amount of mayonnaise, top with 2 slices of turkey, keeping the edges neat, and then top with a couple of slices of tomato. Season to taste with salt and pepper. Add another slice of toast and top with 2 pancetta rashers and 1 lettuce leaf. Season to taste again with salt and pepper, add a little more mayonnaise, then top with the final piece of toast. Push a cocktail stick or a decorative sparkler through a stuffed olive, and then push this through the sandwich to hold it together.

Blinis with Prawns & *Wasabi Cream*

SERVES 6

350 g/12 oz plain flour
125 g/4½ oz buckwheat flour
2 tsp easy-blend dried yeast
600 ml/1 pint full-fat milk, warmed
6 eggs, separated
3 tbsp unsalted butter, melted
5 tbsp soured cream
50 g/1¾ oz clarified butter
salt

WASABI CREAM
200 ml/7 fl oz soured cream or
   crème fraîche
½ tsp wasabi paste, or to taste

TO SERVE
300 g/10½ oz cooked prawns,
   peeled and deveined
50 g/1¾ oz pickled ginger,
   thinly sliced
2 tbsp fresh coriander leaves

★ Sift the flours together into a large bowl and stir in the yeast. Make a hollow in the centre and add the milk, then gradually beat in the flour until you have a smooth batter. Cover and chill in the refrigerator overnight.

★ Two hours before you need the blinis, remove the bowl from the refrigerator and leave the batter for 1 hour 20 minutes to return to room temperature. Beat in the egg yolks, melted butter and soured cream. In a separate bowl, whisk the egg whites until stiff, then gradually fold into the batter. Cover and leave to rest for 30 minutes.

★ Meanwhile, make the wasabi cream. Mix the soured cream and wasabi paste together in a small bowl until completely combined. Taste and add a little more wasabi paste if you like it hotter. Season to taste with salt only, cover and chill in the refrigerator.

★ To cook the blinis, heat a little of the clarified butter in a non-stick frying pan over a medium-high heat. When hot and sizzling, drop in 3–4 tablespoonfuls of the batter, spaced well apart, and cook until puffed up and tiny bubbles appear around the edges. Flip them over and cook for a few more minutes on the other side. Remove from the pan and keep warm while you cook the remaining batter.

★ To serve, spoon a little of the wasabi cream on to a blini, add 1 or 2 prawns and a little ginger, then scatter with a few coriander leaves.

Smoked Salmon
Risotto

SERVES 4

50 g/1¾ oz unsalted butter
1 onion, finely chopped
½ small fennel bulb,
   very finely chopped
500 g/1 lb 2 oz arborio or
   carnaroli rice
300 ml/10 fl oz white wine
   or vermouth
1.2 litres/2 pints hot fish stock
150 g/5½ oz hot smoked
   salmon flakes
150 g/5½ oz smoked
   salmon slices
2 tbsp fresh chervil leaves or
   chopped flat-leaf parsley
salt and pepper

★ Melt half the butter in a large saucepan over a medium heat, add the onion and fennel and cook, stirring frequently, for 5–8 minutes until transparent and soft. Add the rice and stir well to coat the grains in the butter. Cook, stirring, for 3 minutes, then add the wine, stir and leave to simmer until most of the liquid has been absorbed.

★ With the stock simmering in a separate saucepan, add 1 ladleful to the rice and stir well. Cook, stirring constantly, until nearly all the liquid has been absorbed before adding another ladleful of stock. Continue to add the remaining stock in the same way until the rice is cooked al dente and most or all of the stock has been added.

★ Remove from the heat and stir in the two types of salmon and the remaining butter, season to taste with salt and pepper and serve scattered with the chervil or parsley.

COOK'S NOTE

★ This risotto can be made with cooked prawns or other seafood - try it with crabmeat and saffron.

Roast Squash with *Cranberries*

SERVES 4

4 acorn or small butternut squash
100 g/3½ oz basmati rice
50 g/1¾ oz wild rice
25 g/1 oz butter
1 tbsp olive oil, plus extra
    for oiling
1 red onion, thinly sliced
2 garlic cloves, crushed
100 g/3½ oz dried cranberries
50 g/1¾ oz pine kernels, toasted
2 tbsp fresh parsley,
    finely chopped
whole nutmeg, for grating
70 g/2½ oz fresh white or
    wholemeal breadcrumbs
25 g/1 oz Parmesan cheese,
    finely grated
butter, for dotting
salt and pepper

★ If using acorn squash, cut through the centre and trim the stalk and root so that the squash will stand upright securely, then scoop out and discard the seeds. If using butternut squash, cut lengthways in half and scoop out and discard the seeds. Place the prepared squash on an oiled baking sheet.

★ Cook the two types of rice separately according to the packet instructions and drain well.

★ Meanwhile, preheat the oven to 190°C/375°F/Gas Mark 5. Melt the butter with the oil in a frying pan over a medium heat, add the onion and garlic and cook, stirring frequently, for 8 minutes, or until transparent and soft.

★ Tip all the cooked rice and the cooked onion and garlic into a bowl. Add the cranberries, pine kernels and parsley, grate in a little nutmeg and season to taste with salt and pepper. Mix together well.

★ Carefully divide the stuffing mixture between the squash, then top with the breadcrumbs and Parmesan cheese and dot with butter. Bake in the preheated oven for 50 minutes, then serve hot.

COOK'S NOTE

★ You can vary the stuffing ingredients and use other nuts such as walnuts or almonds and replace the cranberries with chopped ready-to-eat dried apricots.

Chestnut, Madeira &

Mushroom Tarts

MAKES 12

PASTRY
100 g/3½ oz unsalted butter,
    chilled and diced, plus
    extra for greasing
225 g/8 oz plain flour, plus extra
    for dusting
pinch of salt

FILLING
25 g/1 oz unsalted butter
1 tsp olive oil
1 shallot, finely chopped
1 garlic clove, crushed
8 cooked chestnuts, peeled and
    roughly chopped
200 g/7 oz chestnut mushrooms,
    chopped
2 tbsp Madeira
150 ml/5 fl oz double cream
1 egg, plus 1 egg yolk
salt and pepper
chopped fresh parsley, to serve

★ Lightly grease a 7.5-cm/3-inch, 12-hole muffin tin with butter. Sift the flour into a large bowl, add the salt and rub in the remaining butter until the mixture resembles breadcrumbs. Add a little cold water – just enough to bring the dough together. Knead the dough briefly on a floured work surface.

★ Divide the pastry in half. Roll out 1 piece of pastry and, using a 9-cm/3½-inch plain pastry cutter, cut out 6 rounds, then roll each round into a 12-cm/4½-inch round. Repeat with the remaining pastry until you have 12 rounds of pastry, then use to line the muffin tin. Chill in the refrigerator for 30 minutes.

★ Meanwhile, preheat the oven to 200°C/400°F/Gas Mark 6 and make the filling. Melt the butter with the oil in a small frying pan over a low heat, add the shallot and garlic and cook, stirring occasionally, for 5–8 minutes until the shallot is transparent and soft. Add the chestnuts and mushrooms and cook, stirring, for 2 minutes, then add the Madeira and simmer for 2 minutes.

★ Line the pastry cases with baking paper and fill with baking beans, then bake in the preheated oven for 10 minutes. Carefully lift out the paper and beans, and reduce the oven temperature to 190°C/375°F/Gas Mark 5. Stir the cream, whole egg and egg yolk into the mushroom mixture and season well with salt and pepper. Divide between the pastry cases and bake for 10 minutes. Leave to cool in the tin for 5 minutes, then carefully remove from the tin, scatter with chopped parsley and serve.

Double Cheese

MAKES 6

25 g/1 oz butter, plus extra
   for greasing
2 tbsp finely grated Parmesan
   cheese
175 ml/6 fl oz milk
25 g/1 oz self-raising flour
whole nutmeg, for grating
100 g/3½ oz soft goat's cheese
70 g/2½ oz mature Cheddar
   cheese, grated
2 large eggs, separated
salt and pepper

★ Preheat the oven to 200°C/400°F/Gas Mark 6. Put a baking sheet in the oven to warm. Generously grease the inside of 6 small ramekins with butter, add half the Parmesan cheese and shake to coat the butter.

★ Warm the milk in a small saucepan. Melt the remaining butter in a separate saucepan over a medium heat. Add the flour, stir well to combine and cook, stirring, for 2 minutes until smooth. Add a little of the warmed milk and stir until absorbed. Continue to add the milk a little at a time, stirring constantly, until you have a rich, smooth sauce. Season to taste with salt and pepper, and grate in a little nutmeg. Add the cheeses to the sauce and stir until well combined and melted.

★ Remove from the heat and leave the sauce to cool a little, then add the egg yolks and stir to combine. In a separate bowl, whisk the egg whites until stiff. Fold a tablespoonful of the egg whites into the cheese sauce, then gradually fold in the remaining egg whites. Spoon into the prepared ramekins and scatter over the remaining Parmesan cheese.

★ Place the ramekins on the hot baking sheet and bake in the preheated oven for 15 minutes until puffed up and brown. Remove from the oven and serve immediately. The soufflés will collapse quite quickly when taken from the oven, so have your serving plates ready to take the soufflés to the table.

COOK'S NOTE

★ You can vary the cheeses, but always choose a full-flavoured, hard cheese to complement the goat's cheese.

Main Courses &

Accompaniments

Roast Turkey with

Bread Sauce

SERVES 8

1 quantity Chestnut and
   Sausage Stuffing
one 5-kg/11-lb turkey
40 g/1½ oz butter

BREAD SAUCE
1 onion, peeled
4 cloves
600 ml/1 pint milk
115 g/4 oz fresh white
   breadcrumbs
55 g/2 oz butter
salt and pepper

✦ Preheat the oven to 220°C/425°F/Gas Mark 7. Spoon the stuffing into the neck cavity of the turkey and close the flap of skin with a skewer. Place the bird in a large roasting tin and rub it all over with the butter. Roast in the preheated oven for 1 hour, then lower the oven temperature to 180°C/350°F/Gas Mark 4 and roast for a further 2½ hours. You may need to pour off the fat from the roasting tin occasionally.

✦ Meanwhile, make the bread sauce. Stud the onion with the cloves, then place in a saucepan with the milk, breadcrumbs and butter. Bring just to boiling point over a low heat, then remove from the heat and leave to stand in a warm place to infuse. Just before serving, remove the onion and cloves and reheat the sauce gently, beating well with a wooden spoon. Season to taste with salt and pepper.

✦ Check that the turkey is cooked by inserting a skewer or the point of a sharp knife into the thigh – if the juices run clear, it is ready. Transfer the bird to a carving board, cover loosely with foil and leave to rest.

✦ Carve the turkey and serve with the warm bread sauce.

Yuletide Goose with
Honey & Pears

SERVES 4–6

one 3.5-4.5-kg/7¾-10-lb
  oven-ready goose
1 tsp salt
4 pears
1 tbsp lemon juice
4 tbsp butter
2 tbsp honey

★ Preheat the oven to 220°C/425°F/Gas Mark 7. Rinse the goose and pat dry. Use a fork to prick the skin all over, then rub with the salt. Place the bird upside down on a rack in a roasting tin. Roast in the preheated oven for 30 minutes. Drain off the fat. Turn the bird over and roast for 15 minutes. Drain off the fat.

★ Reduce the heat to 180°C/350°F/Gas Mark 4 and roast for 15 minutes per 450 g/1 lb. Cover with foil 15 minutes before the end of the cooking time. Check that the bird is cooked by inserting a knife between the legs and body. If the juices run clear, it is cooked. Remove from the oven. Transfer the goose to a warmed serving platter, cover loosely with foil and leave to rest.

★ Peel and halve the pears, then brush with the lemon juice. Melt the butter and honey in a saucepan over a low heat, then add the pears. Cook, stirring, for 5-10 minutes until tender. Remove from the heat, arrange the pears around the goose and pour the sweet juices over the bird, then serve.

COOK'S NOTE

★ 'Christmas is coming and the goose is getting fat' - and they do look like extremely big birds. However, there is proportionately a lot less meat on a goose than on a turkey or chicken because a goose's rib cage is so large.

Glazed
Gammon

SERVES 8

one 4-kg/8¾-lb gammon joint
1 apple, cored and chopped
1 onion, chopped
300 ml/10 fl oz dry cider
6 black peppercorns
1 bouquet garni
1 bay leaf
about 50 cloves
4 tbsp Demerara sugar

✶ Put the gammon in a large saucepan and add enough cold water to cover. Bring to the boil and skim off the scum that rises to the surface. Reduce the heat and simmer for 30 minutes. Drain the gammon and return to the saucepan. Add the apple, onion, cider, peppercorns, bouquet garni, bay leaf and a few of the cloves. Pour in enough fresh water to cover and return to the boil. Reduce the heat, cover and simmer for 3 hours 20 minutes.

✶ Preheat the oven to 200°C/400°F/Gas Mark 6. Take the saucepan off the heat and set aside to cool slightly. Remove the gammon from the cooking liquid and, while it is still warm, loosen the rind with a sharp knife, then peel it off and discard. Score the fat into diamond shapes and stud with the remaining cloves. Place the gammon on a rack in a roasting tin and sprinkle with the sugar. Roast in the oven, basting occasionally with the cooking liquid, for 20 minutes. Serve hot, or cold later.

COOK'S NOTE

✶ You can buy ready-made bouquet garni in little sachets like teabags. However, fresh herbs are much more flavoursome. Tie together 2-3 fresh parsley sprigs, 1 fresh thyme sprig and a fresh bay leaf into a bundle. For extra flavour, tie them together with a strip of celery rather than string.

Roast Pheasant with
Wine & Herbs

SERVES 4

100 g/3½ oz butter,
   slightly softened
1 tbsp chopped fresh thyme
1 tbsp chopped fresh parsley
2 oven-ready young pheasants
4 tbsp vegetable oil
125 ml/4 fl oz red wine
salt and pepper
game chips (see Cook's Note,
   below), to serve

★ Preheat the oven to 190°C/375°F/Gas Mark 5. Put the butter in a small bowl and mix in the chopped herbs. Lift the skins off the pheasants, taking care not to tear them, and push the herb butter under the skins. Season to taste with salt and pepper. Pour the oil into a roasting tin, add the pheasants and roast in the preheated oven for 45 minutes, basting occasionally. Remove from the oven, pour over the wine, then return to the oven and cook for a further 15 minutes, or until cooked through. Check that each bird is cooked by inserting a knife between the legs and body. If the juices run clear, they are cooked.

★ Remove the pheasants from the oven, cover loosely with foil and leave to rest for 15 minutes. Serve on a warmed serving platter surrounded with game chips.

COOK'S NOTE

★ To make game chips, peel 650 g/1 lb 7 oz potatoes and cut into wafer-thin slices. Immediately place in a bowl of cold water. Heat sunflower or corn oil in a deep-fryer to 190°C/375°F, or until a cube of day-old bread browns in 30 seconds. Drain the potato slices and pat dry with kitchen paper. Deep-fry, in batches, for 2–3 minutes, stirring to prevent them from sticking, and remove with a slotted spoon. Drain on kitchen paper and keep warm while you cook the remaining slices.

Festive Beef
Wellington

SERVES 4

750 g/1 lb 10 oz thick beef fillet
2 tbsp butter
2 tbsp vegetable oil
1 garlic clove, chopped
1 onion, chopped
175 g/6 oz chestnut mushrooms,
   thinly sliced
1 tbsp chopped fresh sage
350 g/12 oz puff pastry,
   thawed if frozen
1 egg, beaten
salt and pepper

★ Preheat the oven to 220°C/425°F/Gas Mark 7. Put the beef in a roasting tin, spread with the butter and season to taste with salt and pepper. Roast in the preheated oven for 30 minutes, then remove from the oven.

★ Meanwhile, heat the oil in a saucepan over a medium heat. Add the garlic and onion and cook, stirring, for 3 minutes. Stir in salt and pepper to taste, the mushrooms and the sage and cook, stirring frequently, for 5 minutes. Remove from the heat.

★ Roll out the pastry into a rectangle large enough to enclose the beef, then place the beef in the centre and spread the mushroom mixture over it. Bring the long sides of the pastry together over the beef and seal with beaten egg. Tuck the short ends over (trim away excess pastry) and seal. Place on a baking sheet, seam-side down. Make 2 slits in the top. Decorate with dough shapes and brush with egg. Bake for 40 minutes. Remove from the oven, cut into thick slices and serve.

COOK'S NOTE

★ Frozen pastry should be thawed before use, but make sure that it is well chilled in the refrigerator before rolling out. This helps to ensure that the layers puff up during cooking. If the pastry browns too quickly in the oven, cover with foil.

Poached
Salmon

SERVES 8–12

4 litres/7 pints water
6 tbsp white wine vinegar
1 large onion, sliced
2 carrots, sliced
1½ tbsp salt
1 tsp black peppercorns
one 2.7-kg/6-lb salmon, cleaned,
    with gills and eyes removed

TO SERVE
green salad leaves
1 cucumber, thinly sliced
lemon wedges

✶ To make a court-bouillon (stock) in which to poach the fish, put the water, vinegar, onion, carrots, salt and peppercorns in a large fish kettle or covered roasting tin and bring to the boil. Reduce the heat and simmer for 20 minutes. Remove the trivet (if using a fish kettle) and lay the salmon on it. Lower it into the court-bouillon, cover, return to simmering point and cook for 5 minutes. Turn off the heat and leave the fish, covered, to cool in the liquid.

✶ When the fish is cold, lift it out of the kettle on the trivet and drain well. Using 2 fish slices, carefully transfer to a board. Using a sharp knife, remove the head, then slit the skin along the backbone and peel off. Carefully turn the fish over and peel off the skin on the other side.

✶ To serve, line a serving platter with green salad leaves and cucumber and carefully transfer the salmon to the platter. Serve with lemon wedges.

COOK'S NOTE

✶ This easy dish is a great choice for a Christmas Eve dinner party or for a cold buffet on Christmas day. It is prepared in advance and provides a welcome contrast to the prodigious quantities of meat often consumed at this time of year. It also looks and tastes rather special.

Duck with Madeira &

Blueberry Sauce

SERVES 4

4 duck breasts (skin left on)
4 garlic cloves, chopped
grated rind and juice of 1 orange
1 tbsp chopped fresh parsley
salt and pepper

MADEIRA AND
BLUEBERRY SAUCE
150 g/5½ oz blueberries
250 ml/9 fl oz Madeira
1 tbsp redcurrant jelly

TO SERVE
new potatoes
selection of green vegetables

✳ Use a sharp knife to make several shallow diagonal cuts in each duck breast. Put the duck in a glass bowl with the garlic, orange rind and juice, and the parsley. Season to taste with salt and pepper and stir well. Turn the duck in the mixture until thoroughly coated. Cover the bowl with clingfilm and leave in the refrigerator to marinate for at least 1 hour.

✳ Heat a dry, non-stick frying pan over a medium heat. Add the duck breasts and cook for 4 minutes, then turn them over and cook for a further 4 minutes, or according to taste. Remove from the heat, cover the frying pan and leave to stand for 5 minutes.

✳ Halfway through the cooking time, put the blueberries, Madeira and redcurrant jelly into a separate saucepan. Bring to the boil. Reduce the heat and simmer for 10 minutes, then remove from the heat.

✳ Slice the duck breasts and transfer to warmed serving plates. Serve with the sauce poured over and accompanied by new potatoes and a selection of green vegetables.

COOK'S NOTE

✳ Duck has a reputation for being a very fatty meat, but modern breeders are producing much leaner birds these days. The meat, therefore, needs careful cooking to prevent it from drying out and losing its texture.

Chicken
Roulades

SERVES 6

6 skinless, boneless chicken
    breasts, about 175 g/6 oz each
200 g/7 oz fresh chicken mince
1 tbsp olive oil
2 shallots, roughly chopped
1 garlic clove, crushed
150 ml/5 fl oz double cream
3 fresh sage leaves, chopped
1 tbsp chopped fresh parsley
1 tbsp cognac or sherry
1 tbsp vegetable oil
18 pancetta rashers
1 dessertspoon plain flour
200 ml/7 fl oz white wine
200 ml/7 fl oz chicken stock
salt and pepper
Parsnip and Potato Rösti, to serve

✦ Place a chicken breast between 2 pieces of clingfilm and, using a rolling pin, flatten the breast as evenly as possible. Trim off the rough edges to make a neat square. Repeat with the remaining breasts, cover and chill in the refrigerator.

✦ Meanwhile, chop the chicken trimmings and mix with the mince in a bowl. Heat the olive oil in a small frying pan over a medium heat, add the shallots and garlic and cook, stirring frequently, for 5 minutes. Add to the mince with the cream, herbs and cognac and mix together thoroughly. Season to taste with salt and pepper, cover and chill in the refrigerator for 15 minutes.

✦ Bring a large saucepan of water to the boil, then reduce to a simmer. Divide the mince mixture between the breasts, spread to within 1 cm/½ inch of the edge, and then roll each breast up to form a sausage shape. Wrap each roll tightly in kitchen foil, securing both ends. Poach in the simmering water for 20 minutes, remove with a slotted spoon and leave to cool completely.

✦ Meanwhile, preheat the oven to 190°C/375°F/Gas Mark 5. Put the vegetable oil in a roasting tin and heat in the oven. Remove the kitchen foil and wrap each roulade tightly in 3 pancetta rashers. Carefully roll in the hot oil, then roast in the oven for 25-30 minutes, turning twice, until they are browned and crisp.

✦ Remove the roulades from the tin and keep warm. Place the tin on the hob, add the flour and stir well with a wooden spoon to form a smooth paste. Gradually whisk in the wine and stock. Leave to bubble for 4-5 minutes, then season to taste. Slice the roulades and serve with rösti and with the gravy.

Traditional
Roast Chicken

SERVES 6

one 2.25-kg/5-lb free-range
    chicken
55 g/2 oz butter
2 tbsp chopped fresh lemon thyme
1 lemon, quartered
125 ml/4 fl oz white wine
salt and pepper
6 fresh thyme sprigs, to garnish

★ Preheat the oven to 220°C/425°F/Gas Mark 7. Make sure the chicken is clean, wiping it inside and out with kitchen paper, and place in a roasting tin. In a bowl, soften the butter with a fork, mix in the thyme and season well with salt and pepper. Butter the chicken all over with the herb butter, inside and out, and place the lemon pieces inside the body cavity. Pour the wine over the chicken.

★ Roast in the centre of the preheated oven for 20 minutes. Reduce the temperature to 190°C/375°F/Gas Mark 5 and roast for a further 1¼ hours, basting frequently. Cover with foil if the skin begins to brown too much. If the tin dries out, add a little more wine or water.

★ Test that the chicken is cooked by piercing the thickest part of the leg with a sharp knife or skewer and making sure the juices run clear. Remove from the oven. Transfer the chicken to a warmed serving plate, cover loosely with foil and leave to rest for 10 minutes before carving. Place the roasting tin on the top of the stove and bubble the pan juices gently over a low heat until they have reduced and are thick and glossy. Season to taste with salt and pepper. Serve the chicken with the pan juices and scatter with the thyme sprigs.

COOK'S NOTE

★ Chicken has become a well-established favourite in recent years, although it was once seen as quite exclusive. Simply roasted, with plenty of thyme and lemon, chicken produces a succulent gastronomic feast for many occasions. You can stuff your chicken with a traditional stuffing, such as sage and onion, or with fruit like apricots and prunes, but often the best way is to keep it simple. If you do stuff the chicken, remember to stuff just the neck end, not the whole cavity, or the bird might not cook all the way through.

Herbed Salmon with
Hollandaise Sauce

SERVES 4

4 salmon fillets, about 175 g/
   6 oz each, skin removed
2 tbsp olive oil
1 tbsp chopped fresh dill
1 tbsp snipped fresh chives,
   plus extra to garnish
salt and pepper

HOLLANDAISE SAUCE
3 egg yolks
1 tbsp water
225 g/8 oz butter, cut into
   small cubes
juice of 1 lemon
salt and pepper

TO SERVE
freshly cooked sprouting broccoli
sesame seeds

✶ Preheat the grill to medium. Rinse the fish fillets under cold running water and pat dry with kitchen paper. Season to taste with salt and pepper. Combine the oil with the dill and chives in a bowl, then brush the mixture over the fish. Transfer to the grill and cook for 6–8 minutes, turning once and brushing with more oil and herb mixture, until cooked to your taste.

✶ Meanwhile, make the sauce. Put the egg yolks in a heatproof bowl over a saucepan of gently simmering water (or use a double boiler). Add the water and season to taste with salt and pepper. Reduce the heat until the water in the saucepan is barely simmering and whisk constantly until the mixture begins to thicken. Whisk in the butter, one piece at a time, until the mixture is thick and shiny. Whisk in the lemon juice, then remove from the heat.

✶ Remove the salmon from the grill and transfer to warmed individual serving plates. Pour the sauce over the fish and garnish with snipped fresh chives. Serve immediately on a bed of sprouting broccoli, garnished with sesame seeds.

COOK'S NOTE

✶ Do not allow the base of the bowl to touch the surface of the water when you are making the sauce, or the egg yolks may curdle. It is also important that the water is barely simmering rather than boiling vigorously.

Mixed Nut Roast with

Cranberry Sauce

SERVES 4

2 tbsp butter, plus extra
   for greasing
2 garlic cloves, chopped
1 large onion, chopped
50 g/1¾ oz pine kernels, toasted
75 g/2¾ oz hazelnuts, toasted
50 g/1¾ oz walnuts, ground
50 g/1¾ oz cashew nuts, ground
100 g/3½ oz fresh wholemeal
   breadcrumbs
1 egg, lightly beaten
2 tbsp chopped fresh thyme
250 ml/9 fl oz vegetable stock
salt and pepper
fresh thyme sprigs, to garnish
Brussels sprouts, to serve

CRANBERRY SAUCE
175 g/6 oz fresh cranberries
100 g/3½ oz caster sugar
300 ml/10 fl oz red wine
1 cinnamon stick

★ Preheat the oven to 180°C/350°F/Gas Mark 4. Grease a loaf tin with butter and line it with greaseproof paper. Melt the remaining butter in a saucepan over a medium heat. Add the garlic and onion and cook, stirring, for 5 minutes, until softened. Remove from the heat. Grind the pine kernels and hazelnuts. Stir all the nuts into the saucepan, add the breadcrumbs, egg, thyme and stock and season to taste with salt and pepper.

★ Spoon the mixture into the loaf tin and level the surface. Cook in the preheated oven for 30 minutes, or until cooked through and golden. The loaf is cooked when a skewer inserted into the centre comes out clean.

★ Halfway through the cooking time, make the sauce. Put all the ingredients in a saucepan and bring to the boil. Reduce the heat and simmer gently, stirring occasionally, for 15 minutes.

★ To serve, remove the sauce from the heat and discard the cinnamon stick. Remove the nut roast from the oven and turn out onto a warmed serving dish. Garnish with thyme sprigs and serve with the sauce and Brussels sprouts.

COOK'S NOTE

★ Nuts contain a lot of oil and will turn rancid if they are stored too long. Buy them in small quantities, store in airtight containers and keep an eye on the 'use by' dates. It is probably worth buying fresh nuts for this festive treat.

Steak with Pancakes &

Mustard Sauce

SERVES 6

vegetable oil, for frying
6 fillet steaks, about
    150 g/5½ oz each
1 tbsp olive oil
1 tsp unsalted butter
200 ml/7 fl oz crème fraîche
2 tsp wholegrain mustard
2 tbsp snipped fresh chives
salt and pepper

PANCAKES
400 g/14 oz potatoes
55 g/2 oz self-raising flour
½ tsp baking powder
200 ml/7 fl oz milk
2 eggs, beaten

★ To make the pancakes, cook the potatoes in their skins in a large saucepan of boiling water until tender. Drain and leave until cool enough to handle. Peel, then pass through a potato ricer, or mash and press through a sieve, into a bowl.

★ Sift the flour and baking powder over the potatoes, then add a little of the milk and mix well. Add the remaining milk and the eggs and beat well to make a smooth batter.

★ Heat a little vegetable oil in a 20-cm/8-inch non-stick frying pan over a medium heat. Add a ladleful of the batter to cover the base of the pan and cook until little bubbles appear on the surface. Turn over and cook for a further minute, or until nicely browned, then turn out and keep warm. Repeat until you have cooked 6 pancakes.

★ Season the steaks to taste with salt and pepper. Heat the olive oil and butter in a non-stick frying pan over a high heat until sizzling. Add the fillet steaks and cook to your liking, then remove from the pan and keep warm. Add the crème fraîche and mustard to the pan, stir and heat through. Season well with salt and pepper. Serve each steak with a folded pancake and some sauce, scattered with a few snipped chives.

COOK'S NOTE

★ The pancakes can also make a vegetarian or non-meat main course, stuffed with some creamed spinach or smoked fish and soured cream.

Apple & Date
Chutney

MAKES ONE 300-G/10½-OZ JAR

175 ml/6 fl oz cider vinegar
1 shallot, finely chopped
1 cooking apple, peeled, cored
   and chopped
¼ tsp ground allspice
300 g/10½ oz Medjool dates,
   stoned and chopped
5 tbsp honey

★ Put the vinegar, shallot, apple and allspice in a saucepan and bring to the boil. Reduce the heat and simmer for 5-8 minutes. Add the dates and honey and cook for 8-10 minutes until the dates are soft and the liquid is syrupy.

★ Remove from the heat and leave to cool. Serve straight away or pack into sterilized jars and store in the refrigerator.

COOK'S NOTE

★ Chutney makes a lovely Christmas gift. Simply tie a ribbon around the lid of the jar and add a decorative label with the date you made it – it will last for 6 weeks in the refrigerator.

Festive Jewelled
Rice

SERVES 6

250 g/9 oz basmati rice
70 g/2½ oz red or wild rice
70 g/2½ oz ready-to-eat
   dried apricots
25 g/1 oz almonds, blanched
25 g/1 oz hazelnuts, toasted
1 fresh red chilli, deseeded and
   finely chopped
seeds of 1 pomegranate
1 tbsp finely chopped fresh parsley
1 tbsp finely chopped fresh mint
1 tbsp finely snipped fresh chives
2 tbsp white wine vinegar
6 tbsp extra virgin olive oil
1 shallot, finely chopped
salt and pepper

★ Cook the two types of rice separately according to the packet instructions. Drain and leave to cool, then tip into a large bowl.

★ Chop the apricots and nuts and add to the rice with the chilli, pomegranate seeds and the herbs. Mix together well.

★ Just before you are ready to serve, whisk the vinegar, oil and shallot together in a jug and season well with salt and pepper. Pour the dressing over the rice and mix well. Pile into a serving dish.

COOK'S NOTE

★ You can use other dried fruits or nuts in this dish and exclude the chilli if you prefer. Top with a few sliced salad onions for extra crunch.

Wild Mushroom
Filo Parcels

SERVES 6

30 g/1 oz dried porcini mushrooms
70 g/2½ oz butter
1 shallot, finely chopped
1 garlic clove, crushed
100 g/3½ oz chestnut
    mushrooms, sliced
100 g/3½ oz white cap
    mushrooms, sliced
200 g/7 oz wild mushrooms,
    roughly chopped
150 g/5½ oz basmati rice,
    cooked and cooled
2 tbsp dry sherry
1 tbsp soy sauce or
    mushroom sauce
1 tbsp chopped fresh
    flat-leaf parsley
18 sheets filo pastry,
    thawed if frozen
vegetable oil, for oiling
350 ml/12 fl oz crème fraîche
50 ml/2 fl oz Madeira
salt and pepper

✷ Put the dried mushrooms in a heatproof bowl and just cover with boiling water. Leave to soak for 20 minutes.

✷ Meanwhile, melt half the butter in a large frying pan over a low heat, add the shallot and garlic and cook, stirring occasionally, for 5-8 minutes until the shallot is transparent and soft. Add all the fresh mushrooms and cook, stirring, for 2-3 minutes.

✷ Preheat the oven to 200°C/400°F/Gas Mark 6. Drain the dried mushrooms, reserving the soaking liquid, roughly chop and add to the frying pan with the rice, sherry, soy sauce and parsley. Season well with salt and pepper, mix together well and simmer until most of the liquid has evaporated.

✷ Melt the remaining butter in a small saucepan. Lay 1 sheet of filo pastry on a work surface and brush with melted butter. Put another sheet on top and brush with butter, then top with a third sheet. Spoon some of the mushroom mixture into the centre, then fold in the edges to form a parcel. Use a little more of the melted butter to make sure that the edges are secure. Repeat to make 6 parcels.

✷ Place the parcels on a lightly oiled baking sheet and brush with the remaining melted butter. Bake in the preheated oven for 25-30 minutes until golden.

✷ Meanwhile, to make the sauce, heat the reserved soaking liquid in a saucepan, add the crème fraîche and Madeira and stir over a low heat until heated through. Season to taste with salt and pepper and serve with the parcels.

Parsnip & Potato
Rösti

SERVES 6

2 large potatoes
2 parsnips
olive oil, goose fat or lard,
    for frying
salt and pepper

★ Peel and grate the potatoes and parsnips on to a clean tea towel. Squeeze out any excess liquid, then spread out on to another clean tea towel or kitchen paper and leave to stand for 10 minutes.

★ Put the potatoes and parsnips in a bowl, mix together and season to taste with salt and pepper. Heat a little oil in a non-stick frying pan over a medium-high heat. Add a spoonful of the potato mixture, flatten with the back of a spoon to form a rösti and cook for 3-5 minutes until brown and crisp. Carefully turn over and cook for a further 2-3 minutes. Remove and drain on kitchen paper. Keep warm while you cook the remaining parsnip and potato mixture.

COOK'S NOTE

★ Rösti are also delicious for breakfast with a poached egg and some grilled pancetta, or with smoked salmon and soured cream and chives.

Perfect Roast

Potatoes

SERVES 8

70 g/2½ oz goose or duck fat
   or 5 tbsp olive oil
1 kg/2 lb 4 oz even-sized potatoes,
   peeled
coarse sea salt
8 fresh rosemary sprigs,
   to garnish

★ Preheat the oven to 230°C/450°F/Gas Mark 8. Put the fat in a large roasting tin, sprinkle generously with sea salt and place in the oven.

★ Meanwhile, cook the potatoes in a large saucepan of boiling water for 8-10 minutes until par-boiled. Drain well and, if the potatoes are large, cut them in half. Return the potatoes to the empty saucepan and shake vigorously to roughen their outsides.

★ Arrange the potatoes in a single layer in the hot fat and roast for 45 minutes. If they look as if they are beginning to char around the edges, reduce the oven temperature to 200°C/400°F/Gas Mark 6. Turn the potatoes over and roast for a further 30 minutes until crisp. Serve garnished with rosemary sprigs.

COOK'S NOTE

★ Use floury potatoes, such as King Edward or Maris Piper, for roasting, because these have the best texture. Do not allow them to stand around once they are cooked, or the outsides will turn leathery instead of crisp.

Two-potato
Purée

SERVES 6

2 large orange sweet potatoes
½ tsp vegetable oil
4 potatoes
25 g/1 oz butter
125 ml/4 fl oz double cream
whole nutmeg, for grating
salt and pepper

✹ Preheat the oven to 190°C/375°F/Gas Mark 5. Rub the sweet potatoes with the oil, then bake in the preheated oven for 20-25 minutes until tender.

✹ Meanwhile, peel the potatoes, then cook in a large saucepan of boiling water until tender. Drain well and put in a colander. Cover with a clean tea towel to absorb the steam and leave to stand until cooled. Mash the potatoes or pass through a potato ricer.

✹ Scoop out the flesh from the sweet potatoes and mix well with the potato in a warmed bowl. Discard the sweet potato skins. Melt the butter with the cream in a small saucepan, then pour half over the potato mixture and beat well with a wooden spoon. Add the remaining cream mixture a little at a time until you achieve the consistency you like. Season to taste with salt and pepper, and add a grating of nutmeg. Beat again, then serve.

COOK'S NOTE

✹ If you make the purée in advance, it can be put into a greased gratin dish, dotted with a little extra butter and cooked under the grill or in a low oven until golden on top.

Garlic Mushrooms with
White Wine
& Chestnuts

SERVES 4

55 g/2 oz butter
4 garlic cloves, chopped
200 g/7 oz button mushrooms,
    sliced
200 g/7 oz chestnut mushrooms,
    sliced
4 tbsp dry white wine
100 ml/3½ fl oz double cream
300 g/10½ oz canned whole
    chestnuts, drained
100 g/3½ oz chanterelle
    mushrooms, sliced
salt and pepper
chopped fresh parsley, to garnish

 Melt the butter in a large saucepan over a medium heat. Add the garlic and cook, stirring, for 3 minutes, until softened. Add the button and chestnut mushrooms and cook for 3 minutes.

 Stir in the wine and cream and season to taste with salt and pepper. Cook for 2 minutes, stirring, then add the chestnuts and the chanterelle mushrooms. Cook for a further 2 minutes, stirring, then remove from the heat and transfer to a warmed serving dish. Garnish with chopped fresh parsley and serve.

COOK'S NOTE

 Using three different types of mushrooms enhances both the flavour and texture of this dish. Button mushrooms are very mild, but readily absorb other flavours, such as garlic and wine. Chestnut mushrooms are meatier and have a stronger flavour, while chanterelles are delicate in both texture and flavour.

Brussels Sprouts with

Buttered Chestnuts

SERVES 4

350 g/12 oz Brussels sprouts,
    trimmed
3 tbsp butter
100 g/3½ oz canned whole
    chestnuts
pinch of grated nutmeg
salt and pepper
50 g/1¾ oz flaked almonds,
    to garnish

★ Bring a large saucepan of salted water to the boil. Add the Brussels sprouts and cook for 5 minutes. Drain thoroughly.

★ Melt the butter in a large saucepan over a medium heat. Add the Brussels sprouts and cook, stirring, for 3 minutes, then add the chestnuts and nutmeg. Season to taste with salt and pepper and stir well. Cook for a further 2 minutes, stirring, then remove from the heat. Transfer to a warmed serving dish, scatter over the almonds and serve.

COOK'S NOTE

★ The flaked almonds in this dish add a lovely nutty flavour to the Brussels sprouts, which is superbly complemented by the chestnuts. When buying Brussels sprouts, look for tight buds with bright green-coloured leaves and no sign of yellowing or sliminess. Choose sprouts that are about the same size for even cooking.

Sugar-glazed
Parsnips

SERVES 8

24 small parsnips, peeled
about 1 tsp salt
115 g/4 oz butter
115 g/4 oz soft brown sugar

★ Place the parsnips in a saucepan, add just enough water to cover, then add the salt. Bring to the boil, reduce the heat, cover and simmer for 20-25 minutes, until tender. Drain well.

★ Melt the butter in a heavy frying pan or wok. Add the parsnips and toss well. Sprinkle with the sugar, then cook, stirring frequently to prevent the sugar from sticking to the pan or burning. Cook the parsnips for 10-15 minutes, until golden and glazed. Transfer to a warm serving dish and serve immediately.

COOK'S NOTE

★ When buying parsnips, look for firm roots with no rusty patches and no damage to the skin. Store them in a cool, well-ventilated place for up to 5 days. Try to buy parsnips that are all about the same size, for even cooking.

Honey-glazed Red Cabbage
with Sultanas

SERVES 4

2 tbsp butter
1 garlic clove, chopped
650 g/1 lb 7 oz red cabbage, shredded
150 g/5½ oz sultanas
1 tbsp clear honey
100 ml/3½ fl oz red wine
100 ml/3½ fl oz water

✦ Melt the butter in a large saucepan over a medium heat. Add the garlic and cook, stirring, for 1 minute, until slightly softened.

✦ Add the cabbage and sultanas, then stir in the honey. Cook for 1 minute more. Pour in the wine and water and bring to the boil. Reduce the heat, cover and simmer gently, stirring occasionally, for 45 minutes, or until the cabbage is cooked. Serve hot.

COOK'S NOTE

✦ Red cabbage is a classic accompaniment to game, such as pheasant, and roast pork or gammon. It also goes well with some poultry, notably goose and duck, counteracting the richness of the meat.

Spiced Winter
Vegetables

SERVES 4

4 parsnips, scrubbed and
    trimmed but left unpeeled
4 carrots, scrubbed and
    trimmed but left unpeeled
2 onions, quartered
1 red onion, quartered
3 leeks, trimmed and cut
    into 6-cm/2½-inch slices
6 garlic cloves, left unpeeled
    and whole
6 tbsp extra virgin olive oil
½ tsp mild chilli powder
pinch of paprika
salt and pepper

★ Preheat the oven to 220°C/425°F/Gas Mark 7. Bring a large saucepan of water to the boil.

★ Cut the parsnips and carrots into wedges of similar size. Add them to the saucepan and cook for 5 minutes. Drain thoroughly and place in an ovenproof dish with the onions, leeks and garlic. Pour over the oil, sprinkle in the spices and salt and pepper to taste, then mix until all the vegetables are well coated.

★ Roast in the preheated oven for at least 1 hour. Turn the vegetables from time to time until they are tender and starting to colour. Remove from the oven, transfer to a warmed serving dish and serve immediately.

COOK'S NOTE

★ Providing there is room in the oven, these vegetables are ideal for Christmas lunch, because they offer a selection of different flavours without taking up the entire hob and several saucepans.

Pork, Cranberry &
Herb Stuffing

SERVES 6

1 tbsp vegetable oil, plus extra
   for oiling
1 onion, finely chopped
2 celery sticks, chopped
450 g/1 lb pork sausage meat
50 g/1¾ oz fresh white or
   wholemeal breadcrumbs
50 g/1¾ oz dried cranberries
70 g/2½ oz fresh cranberries
1 tbsp chopped fresh parsley
1 tbsp chopped fresh sage
1 tbsp chopped fresh
   thyme leaves
1 large egg, beaten
salt and pepper

✳ Heat the oil in a heavy-based frying pan over a medium heat, add the onion and celery and cook, stirring frequently, for 10 minutes until the onion is transparent and soft.

✳ Meanwhile, preheat the oven to 190°C/375°F/Gas Mark 5. Break up the sausage meat in a large bowl. Add the breadcrumbs, dried and fresh cranberries and the herbs and mix together well. Add the cooked onion and celery, then the egg. Season well with salt and pepper and mix together thoroughly.

✳ Form the stuffing into balls, place on an oiled baking sheet and bake in the preheated oven for 25 minutes. Alternatively, spoon into 2 foil tins, level the surface and bake for 45 minutes.

COOK'S NOTE

✳ This stuffing can be made in advance and frozen, as long as the sausage meat has not previously been frozen. Thaw thoroughly before cooking.

Chestnut & Sausage

Stuffing

SERVES 6–8

225 g/8 oz pork sausage meat
225 g/8 oz unsweetened
   chestnut purée
85 g/3 oz walnuts, chopped
115 g/4 oz ready-to-eat dried
   apricots, chopped
2 tbsp chopped fresh parsley
2 tbsp snipped fresh chives
2 tsp chopped fresh sage
4–5 tbsp double cream
salt and pepper

★ Combine the sausage meat and chestnut purée in a bowl, then stir in the walnuts, apricots, parsley, chives and sage. Stir in enough cream to make a firm, but not dry, mixture. Season to taste with salt and pepper.

★ If you are planning to stuff a turkey or goose, fill the neck cavity only to ensure the bird cooks all the way through. It is safer and more reliable to cook the stuffing separately, either rolled into small balls and placed on a baking sheet or spooned into an ovenproof dish.

★ Cook the separate stuffing in a preheated oven for 30–40 minutes at 190°C/ 375°F/Gas Mark 5. It should be allowed a longer time to cook if you are roasting a bird at a lower temperature in the same oven.

COOK'S NOTE

★ The combination of nuts, fruit and herbs in this stuffing helps to counteract the richness of traditional Christmas poultry, such as turkey and goose. It also produces an appetizing aroma during cooking.

Cranberry

Sauce

SERVES 8

thinly pared rind and juice
   of 1 lemon
thinly pared rind and juice
   of 1 orange
350 g/12 oz cranberries,
   thawed if frozen
140 g/5 oz caster sugar
2 tbsp arrowroot, mixed
   with 3 tbsp cold water

★ Cut the strips of lemon and orange rind into thin shreds and place in a heavy-based saucepan. If using fresh cranberries, rinse well and remove any stalks. Add the berries, citrus juice and sugar to the saucepan and cook over a medium heat, stirring occasionally, for 5 minutes, or until the berries begin to burst.

★ Strain the juice into a clean saucepan and reserve the cranberries. Stir the arrowroot mixture into the juice, then bring to the boil, stirring constantly, until the sauce is smooth and thickened. Remove from the heat and stir in the reserved cranberries.

★ Transfer the cranberry sauce to a bowl and leave to cool, then cover with clingfilm and chill in the refrigerator.

COOK'S NOTE

★ Turkey and cranberry sauce make a classic Christmas partnership. However, cranberry sauce can also be served to good effect with game, roast duck or chicken, or even some oily fish.

Party Food & *Drinks*

Hot Rum
Punch

SERVES 4.3 LITRES/7½ PINTS

850 ml/1½ pints rum
850 ml/1½ pints brandy
600 ml/1 pint freshly squeezed
   lemon juice
3-4 tbsp caster sugar
2 litres/3½ pints boiling water
slices of fruit, to decorate

Mix together the rum, brandy, lemon juice and 3 tablespoons of the sugar in a punch bowl or large heatproof mixing bowl. Pour in the boiling water and stir well to mix. Taste and add more sugar if required. Decorate with the fruit slices and serve immediately in heatproof glasses with handles.

COOK'S NOTE

This warming drink is a great way to greet guests on Christmas evening and a much-deserved reward for those who venture out for a brisk walk on Boxing Day. Father Christmas probably deserves a glass, too.

Mulled Ale &
Mulled Wine

MULLED ALE
MAKES 2.8 LITRES/5 PINTS

2.5 litres/4½ pints strong ale
300 ml/10 fl oz brandy
2 tbsp caster sugar
large pinch of ground cloves
large pinch of ground ginger

MULLED WINE
MAKES 3.3 LITRES/5¾ PINTS

5 oranges
50 cloves
thinly pared rind and juice
   of 4 lemons
850 ml/1½ pints water
115 g/4 oz caster sugar
2 cinnamon sticks
2 litres/3½ pints red wine
150 ml/5 fl oz brandy

Mulled Ale

★ Put all the ingredients in a heavy-based saucepan and heat gently, stirring, until the sugar has dissolved. Continue to heat so that it is simmering but not boiling. Remove the saucepan from the heat and serve the ale immediately in heatproof glasses.

Mulled Wine

★ Prick the skins of 3 of the oranges all over with a fork and stud with the cloves, then set aside. Thinly pare the rind and squeeze the juice from the remaining oranges.

★ Put the orange rind and juice, lemon rind and juice, water, sugar and cinnamon in a heavy-based saucepan and bring to the boil over a medium heat, stirring occasionally, until the sugar has dissolved. Boil for 2 minutes without stirring, then remove from the heat, stir once and leave to stand for 10 minutes. Strain the liquid into a heatproof jug, pressing down on the contents of the sieve to extract all the juice.

★ Pour the wine into a separate saucepan and add the strained spiced juices, the brandy and the clove-studded oranges. Simmer gently without boiling, then remove the saucepan from the heat. Strain into heatproof glasses and serve the mulled wine immediately.

Cheese *Straws*

MAKES 10–12

115 g/4 oz unsalted butter, plus
   extra for greasing
115 g/4 oz plain flour, plus extra
   for dusting
pinch of salt
pinch of paprika
1 tsp mustard powder
85 g/3 oz Cheddar or Gruyère
   cheese, grated
1 egg, lightly beaten
1–2 tbsp cold water
poppy seeds, for coating

★ Preheat the oven to 200°C/400°F/Gas Mark 6. Lightly grease 2 baking sheets with butter.

★ Sift the flour, salt, paprika and mustard powder into a bowl. Add the remaining butter, cut it into the flour with a knife, then rub in with your fingertips until the mixture resembles breadcrumbs. Stir in the cheese and add half of the beaten egg, then mix in enough water to make a firm dough. The dough may be stored in the freezer. Thaw at room temperature before rolling out.

★ Spread out the poppy seeds on a plate. Turn the dough on to a lightly floured work surface and knead briefly, then roll out. Using a sharp knife, cut into strips measuring 10 x 0.5 cm/4 x ¼ inch. Brush with the remaining beaten egg and roll the straws in the poppy seeds to coat, then arrange them on the baking sheets. Gather up the dough trimmings and re-roll. Stamp out 10-12 rounds with a 6-cm/2½-inch fluted cutter, then stamp out the centres with a 5-cm/2-inch plain cutter. Brush with the egg and place on the baking sheets.

★ Bake in the preheated oven for 10 minutes until golden brown. Leave the cheese straws on the baking sheets to cool slightly, then transfer to wire racks to cool completely. Store in an airtight container. Thread the pastry straws through the pastry rings before serving.

COOK'S NOTE

★ Rather than using poppy seeds, you can brush the cheese straws with mild mustard and sprinkle with a little cayenne pepper before baking. Be careful not to make them too spicy.

Scallops Wrapped

in Pancetta

SERVES 12

12 fresh rosemary sprigs
6 raw scallops, corals removed
12 thin-cut pancetta rashers
salt and pepper

DRESSING
2 tbsp olive oil
1 tbsp white wine vinegar
1 tsp honey

★ First prepare the rosemary by stripping most of the leaves off the stalks, leaving a cluster of leaves at the top. Trim the stalks to about 6 cm/2½ inches long, cutting each tip at the base end at an angle.

★ Cut each scallop in half through the centre to give 2 discs of scallop, wrap each one in a pancetta rasher and, keeping the end tucked under, place on a plate. Cover and chill in the refrigerator for 15 minutes.

★ To make the dressing, whisk the oil, vinegar and honey together in a small bowl and season to taste with salt and pepper.

★ Preheat the grill to high or heat a ridged griddle pan over a high heat. Cook the scallops under the grill or on the griddle pan for 2 minutes on each side until the pancetta is crisp and brown. Spear each one on a prepared rosemary skewer and serve hot, with the dressing as a dip.

COOK'S NOTE

★ These could be served alongside cocktail sausages and angels on horseback (oysters wrapped in pancetta) as delicious hot party snacks.

Piquant Crab
Bites

MAKES 50

100 g/3½ oz fresh white
    breadcrumbs
2 large eggs, separated
200 ml/7 fl oz crème fraîche
1 tsp English mustard powder
500 g/1 lb 2 oz fresh
    white crabmeat
1 tbsp chopped fresh dill
groundnut oil, for frying
salt and pepper
2 limes, quartered, to serve

★ Tip the breadcrumbs into a large bowl. In a separate bowl, whisk the egg yolks with the crème fraîche and mustard powder and add to the breadcrumbs with the crabmeat and dill, season to taste with salt and pepper and mix together well. Cover and chill in the refrigerator for 15 minutes.

★ In a clean bowl, whisk the egg whites until stiff. Lightly fold a tablespoonful of the egg whites into the crab mixture, then fold in the remaining egg whites.

★ Heat 2 tablespoons of oil in a non-stick frying pan over a medium-high heat. Drop in as many teaspoonfuls of the crab mixture as will fit in the frying pan without overcrowding, flatten slightly and cook for 2 minutes, or until brown and crisp. Flip over and cook for a further 1–2 minutes until the undersides are browned. Remove and drain on kitchen paper. Keep warm while you cook the remaining crab mixture, adding more oil to the frying pan if necessary.

★ Serve the crab bites warm with the lime quarters for squeezing over.

COOK'S NOTE

★ These can be made in advance and reheated in a medium oven. They also freeze well, in which case they should be cooked, cooled and then frozen. Thaw thoroughly before reheating.

Leek & Bacon
Tartlets

MAKES 12

PASTRY
225 g/8 oz plain flour
pinch of salt
½ tsp paprika
100 g/3½ oz unsalted butter,
    chilled and diced, plus extra
    for greasing

FILLING
25 g/1 oz unsalted butter
1 tsp olive oil
1 leek, trimmed and chopped
8 unsmoked streaky bacon
    rashers, cut into lardons
2 eggs, beaten
150 ml/5 fl oz double cream
1 tsp snipped fresh chives
salt and pepper

★ Lightly grease a 7.5-cm/3-inch, 12-hole muffin tin with butter. Sift the flour, salt and paprika into a bowl and rub in the remaining butter until the mixture resembles breadcrumbs. Add a very little cold water – just enough to bring the dough together. Knead the dough briefly on a floured work surface.

★ Divide the pastry in half. Roll out 1 piece of pastry and, using a 9-cm/3½-inch plain cutter, cut out 6 rounds, then roll each round into a 12-cm/4½-inch round. Repeat with the other half of the pastry until you have 12 rounds, then use to line the muffin tin. Cover and chill in the refrigerator for 30 minutes.

★ Meanwhile, preheat the oven to 200°C/400°F/Gas Mark 6. To make the filling, melt the butter with the oil in a non-stick frying pan over a medium heat, add the leek and cook, stirring frequently, for 5 minutes until soft. Remove with a slotted spoon and set aside. Add the lardons to the frying pan and cook for 5 minutes, or until crisp. Remove and drain on kitchen paper.

★ Line the pastry cases with baking paper and baking beans and bake in the preheated oven for 10 minutes. Whisk the eggs and cream together in a bowl, season to taste with salt and pepper, then stir in the chives with the cooked leek and bacon. Remove the pastry cases from the oven and carefully lift out the paper and beans. Divide the bacon and leek mixture between the pastry cases and bake for 10 minutes until the tarts are golden and risen. Leave to cool in the tin for 5 minutes, then carefully transfer to a wire rack. Serve warm or cold.

Corn & Parmesan
Fritters

MAKES 25-30

5 fresh corn on the cob
   or 500 g/1 lb 2 oz frozen or
   canned sweetcorn kernels
2 eggs, beaten
4 tbsp plain flour
2 tbsp finely grated
   Parmesan cheese
1 tsp bicarbonate of soda
4 tbsp full-fat milk
vegetable oil, for frying
salt

★ If you are using fresh corn on the cobs, cook them in a large saucepan of boiling water for 7 minutes, then drain well. Stand them on their ends, cut away the kernels and leave to cool. If using frozen sweetcorn kernels, leave to thaw first, or drain canned sweetcorn kernels.

★ Put the sweetcorn kernels in a bowl with the eggs, flour, Parmesan cheese, bicarbonate of soda and a pinch of salt. Mix together, then add the milk and stir together well.

★ Heat the oil to a depth of 4 cm/1½ inches in a deep saucepan to a temperature of 180-190°C/350-375°F, or until a cube of bread browns in 30 seconds. Drop 4 teaspoonfuls of the mixture into the oil at a time and cook for 2 minutes. Turn over and cook for a further minute or so, or until crisp, brown and slightly puffed up. Remove and drain on kitchen paper. Keep warm while you cook the remaining batches of mixture – you may need to add a little more oil between batches and scoop out any stray sweetcorn kernels. Sprinkle with salt to serve.

COOK'S NOTE

★ You could replace the Parmesan cheese with ½ teaspoon of either paprika or chilli powder for extra bite.

Smoked Turkey &

Stuffing Parcels

MAKES 12

12 slices smoked turkey breast
4 tbsp cranberry sauce or jelly
400 g/14 oz cooked and cooled
    sausage-meat stuffing
24 sheets filo pastry, thawed
    if frozen
70 g/2½ oz butter, melted

★ Preheat the oven to 190°C/375°F/Gas Mark 5. Put a non-stick baking sheet into the oven to heat.

★ For each parcel, spread a slice of smoked turkey with a teaspoonful of cranberry sauce, spoon 35 g/1¼ oz of the stuffing into the centre and roll up the turkey slice. Lay 1 sheet of filo pastry on a work surface and brush with a little of the melted butter. Put another sheet on top, then put the rolled-up turkey in the centre. Add a little more cranberry sauce, then carefully fold the filo pastry around the turkey, tucking under the ends to form a neat parcel. Repeat to make 12 parcels.

★ Place the parcels on the hot baking sheet, brush with the remaining melted butter and bake in the preheated oven for 25 minutes until golden. Serve hot.

COOK'S NOTE

★ You can add a few chopped chestnuts or other Christmas leftovers to these parcels, or replace the turkey with cooked chicken.

Desserts & After-dinner Treats

Gingered Brandy

Snaps

MAKES 36

vegetable oil, for greasing
115 g/4 oz unsalted butter
140 g/5 oz golden syrup
115 g/4 oz Demerara sugar
115 g/4 oz plain flour
2 tsp ground ginger
600 ml/1 pint stiffly whipped
   double cream, to serve

★ Preheat the oven to 160°C/325°F/Gas Mark 3. Brush a non-stick baking sheet with oil. Place the butter, syrup and sugar in a saucepan and set over a low heat, stirring occasionally, until melted and combined. Remove the saucepan from the heat and leave to cool slightly. Sift the flour and ground ginger together into the butter mixture and beat until smooth. Spoon 2 teaspoons of the mixture on to the baking sheet, spacing them well apart. Bake for 8 minutes until pale golden brown. Keep the remaining mixture warm. Meanwhile, oil the handle of a wooden spoon.

★ Remove the baking sheet from the oven and leave to stand for 1 minute so that the brandy snaps firm up slightly. Remove 1 with a palette knife and immediately curl it around the handle of the wooden spoon. Once set, carefully slide it off the handle and transfer to a wire rack to cool completely. Repeat with the other brandy snap. Bake the remaining mixture and shape in the same way, using a cool baking sheet each time. Do not be tempted to cook more, or the rounds will set before you have time to shape them. When all the brandy snaps are cool, store in an airtight container.

★ To serve, spoon the whipped cream into a piping bag fitted with a star nozzle. Fill the brandy snaps with cream from both ends.

COOK'S NOTE

★ The unfilled brandy snaps will keep for at least a week in an airtight container. Do not fill them with cream until you are almost ready to serve, or they will become soggy and collapse as guests try to eat them.

Cinnamon Poached Fruits
with Biscuits

SERVES 6

115 g/4 oz ready-to-eat
   dried apricots
115 g/4 oz dried figs, halved
150 g/5½ oz Medjool dates,
   stoned and halved lengthways
115 g/4 oz sultanas
2 cinnamon sticks
2 star anise
5 cardamom pods, crushed
1 tbsp water
500 ml/18 fl oz Beaumes de
   Venise or other dessert wine

ALMOND THINS
125 g/4½ oz ground almonds
175 g/6 oz unrefined caster sugar
3 tbsp finely grated orange rind
50 g/1¾ oz plain flour
3 large egg whites
50 g/1¾ oz flaked almonds,
   toasted
2 tbsp white icing sugar
seeds from 1 pomegranate,
   to decorate
mascarpone cheese or crème
   fraîche, to serve

★ The day before you want to serve, put all the fruit in a saucepan with the cinnamon sticks, star anise and cardamom pods. Add the water and wine, heat very gently to a simmer and poach for 5 minutes. Remove from the heat and remove the cardamom pods and star anise, but leave in the cinnamon sticks. Leave to cool completely, then cover and chill overnight in the refrigerator.

★ Preheat the oven to 180°C/350°F/Gas Mark 4. Line 2 baking sheets with baking paper.

★ To make the biscuits, put the ground almonds in a bowl, add 100 g/3½ oz of the caster sugar, the orange rind and flour and stir well. In a separate bowl, whisk the egg whites until they form soft peaks, then whisk in the remaining caster sugar until the mixture is glossy and stiff. Fold the egg whites into the almond mixture.

★ Place teaspoonfuls of the mixture, spaced well apart, on the baking sheets, then sprinkle over the almonds. Bake in the preheated oven for 12 minutes until puffed up and beginning to brown. Dust with the icing sugar and leave to cool for 10 minutes before transferring to a wire rack to cool completely.

★ To serve, remove the cinnamon sticks from the poached fruit and divide between 6 stemmed glasses. Spoon over a little mascarpone cheese and scatter over the pomegranate seeds. Serve with the almond thins.

Chocolate Chestnut *Roulade*

SERVES 6

6 large eggs, separated
150 g/5½ oz unrefined caster
    sugar
½ tsp vanilla or chocolate extract
50 g/1¾ oz cocoa powder
icing sugar, for dusting
250 ml/9 fl oz double cream
250 g/9 oz sweetened
    chestnut purée
2 tbsp brandy
70 g/2½ oz cooked peeled
    chestnuts, chopped

Preheat the oven to 180°C/350°F/Gas Mark 4. Line a 23 x 45-cm (9 x 17¾-inch) Swiss roll tin with baking paper.

Using an electric whisk, beat the egg yolks, caster sugar and vanilla extract together in a bowl for 10 minutes, or until doubled in volume and pale and fluffy. In a separate bowl, whisk the egg whites until they form soft peaks. Fold a tablespoonful of egg whites into the egg yolk mixture, then gently fold in the remaining egg whites and the cocoa powder.

Spoon the cake mixture into the prepared tin and smooth the surface with a palette knife. Bake in the preheated oven for 20 minutes until risen. Leave to cool in the tin.

Put a large piece of baking paper over a clean tea towel and dust with icing sugar, invert the sponge on to the baking paper and carefully peel away the lining paper. In a clean bowl, whisk the cream until stiff, then stir in the chestnut purée and the brandy. Spread over the sponge, leaving a 2.5-cm/1-inch margin around the edges, and scatter over the chestnuts. Using one end of the tea towel, careful roll up the roulade. Dust with more icing sugar.

COOK'S NOTE

You could replace the chestnuts in the filling with chopped plain chocolate or a few raspberries, if you prefer.

Poached Pears
with Marsala

SERVES 6

6 Comice or other dessert pears,
   peeled but left whole with
   stalks attached
500 ml/18 fl oz Marsala
125 ml/4 fl oz water
1 tbsp soft brown sugar
1 piece of lemon rind or mandarin
   rind
1 vanilla pod
350 ml/12 fl oz double cream
1 tbsp icing sugar

✦ Put the pears in a large saucepan with the Marsala, water, brown sugar and lemon rind and bring gently to the boil, stirring to make sure that the sugar has dissolved. Reduce the heat, cover and simmer for 30 minutes until the pears are tender. Leave the pears to cool in the liquid. Remove the pears from the liquid, cover and chill in the refrigerator.

✦ Discard the lemon rind and leave the liquid to bubble for 15-20 minutes, or until syrupy. Leave to cool.

✦ Cut a thin sliver of flesh from the base of each pear so that they will stand upright. Slit the vanilla pod open and scrape out the seeds into a bowl. Whisk the cream, vanilla seeds and icing sugar together in a bowl until thick. Put each pear on a dessert plate and pour over a little syrup. Serve with the vanilla cream.

COOK'S NOTE

✦ You can add a few pieces of chopped stem ginger to the syrup when cool and serve the pears with some stem ginger or cinnamon ice cream.

Traditional Brandy
Butter

SERVES 6-8

115 g/4 oz unsalted butter,
   at room temperature
55 g/2 oz caster sugar
55 g/2 oz icing sugar, sifted
3 tbsp brandy

★ Cream the butter in a bowl until it is very smooth and soft. Gradually beat in both types of sugar. Add the brandy, a little at a time, beating well after each addition and taking care not to let the mixture curdle.

★ Spread out the butter on a sheet of foil, cover and chill in the refrigerator until firm. Keep chilled until ready to serve.

COOK'S NOTE

★ As an alternative, make a tasty rum butter. Beat the finely grated rind of 1 unwaxed orange into the butter with the two types of sugar and substitute dark or white rum for the brandy, adding it gradually to avoid curdling.

Chocolate Truffle

Selection

MAKES 40-50

225 g/8 oz plain chocolate,
    minimum 70% cocoa solids
175 ml/6 fl oz whipping cream
cocoa powder, icing sugar or
    chopped toasted almonds,
    for coating

Roughly chop the chocolate and put in a large heatproof bowl. Put the cream in a saucepan and bring up to boiling point. Pour over the chocolate and whisk until smooth. Leave to cool at room temperature for 1½–2 hours.

Cover 2 baking sheets with clingfilm or baking paper. Using a teaspoon, take bite-sized scoops of the chocolate mixture and roll in cocoa powder, icing sugar or chopped nuts to form balls, then place on the prepared baking sheets and chill in the refrigerator until set.

COOK'S NOTE

You can also add other flavours to the truffles – add a little brandy, Calvados or dark rum to the mixture before you leave it to set. The truffles could also be covered in milk chocolate or white chocolate – a mixture looks inviting when boxed as a gift.

Dark & White Chocolate

Florentines

MAKES 20

25 g/1 oz unsalted butter,
   plus extra for greasing
70 g/2½ oz unrefined caster sugar
15 g/½ oz plain flour, plus extra
   for dusting
4 tbsp double cream
50 g/1¾ oz whole blanched
   almonds, roughly chopped
50 g/1¾ oz flaked almonds,
   toasted
50 g/1¾ oz mixed peel, chopped
50 g/1¾ oz undyed glacé cherries,
   chopped
50 g/1¾ oz preserved stem ginger,
   drained and chopped
70 g/2½ oz plain chocolate,
   minimum 70% cocoa solids,
   broken into pieces
70 g/2½ oz white chocolate,
   broken into pieces

★ Preheat the oven to 190°C/375°F/Gas Mark 5. Lightly grease 2 baking sheets with butter and dust with flour, shaking to remove any excess.

★ Put the remaining butter, sugar and flour in a small saucepan and heat gently, stirring well, until the mixture has melted. Gradually add the cream, stirring constantly, then add all the remaining ingredients, except the chocolate, and stir thoroughly. Remove from the heat and leave to cool.

★ Drop 5 teaspoonfuls of the mixture on to each of the prepared baking sheets, spaced well apart to allow for spreading, then flatten with the back of a spoon. Bake in the preheated oven for 12–15 minutes. Leave the biscuits to harden on the sheets for 2–3 minutes before transferring to a wire rack. Repeat with the remaining mixture, again using the 2 baking sheets.

★ When the biscuits are completely cool, put the plain chocolate in a heatproof bowl, set the bowl over a saucepan of barely simmering water and heat until melted. Using a teaspoon, spread the base of 10 of the biscuits with the melted chocolate and place chocolate side-up on a wire rack to set. Repeat with the white chocolate and the remaining 10 biscuits.

COOK'S NOTE

★ Use whole candied peel if you can find it and chop it yourself. If you don't like ginger, replace it with angelica or dyed green cherries.

Festive Mince *Pies*

SERVES 16

100 g/3½ oz butter, plus extra
    for greasing
200 g/7 oz plain flour, plus extra
    for dusting
25 g/1 oz icing sugar
1 egg yolk
2-3 tbsp milk, plus extra
    for glazing
300 g/10½ oz mincemeat
icing sugar, for dusting

★ Preheat the oven to 180°C/350°F/Gas Mark 4. Grease a 16-hole tartlet tin with butter. Sift the flour into a bowl. Using your fingertips, rub in the remaining butter until the mixture resembles breadcrumbs. Stir in the sugar and egg yolk. Stir in enough milk to make a soft dough, turn out on to a lightly floured work surface and knead lightly until smooth.

★ Shape the dough into a ball and roll out to a thickness of 1 cm/½ inch. Use fluted cutters to cut out 16 rounds measuring 7 cm/2¾ inches in diameter and use to line the holes in the tartlet tin. Half-fill each pie with mincemeat. Cut out 16 star shapes from the leftover dough, brush with milk and place on top of each pie. Glaze the surface with more milk and bake in the preheated oven for 15 minutes until the pastry is a pale golden colour. Remove from the oven and leave to cool on a wire rack. Dust with icing sugar before serving.

COOK'S NOTE

★ To make your own mincemeat, mix together 450 g/1 lb mixed dried fruit, 115 g/4 oz Demerara sugar, 115 g/4 oz shredded suet, 115 g/4 oz mixed peel, 115 g/4 oz chopped blanched almonds, finely grated rind and juice of 1 lemon, 115 g/4 oz grated apple, 1 teaspoon mixed spice, ½ teaspoon freshly grated nutmeg, ½ teaspoon ground cinnamon and 4 tablespoons brandy. Pack into sterilized jars and seal the lids.

Marzipan-stuffed
Dates

SERVES 6-8

500 g/1 lb 2 oz fresh dates
275 g/9½ oz marzipan

★ Using a small, sharp knife, cut lengthways along the side of each date and carefully remove and discard the stone. Divide the marzipan into the same number of pieces as there are dates and roll each piece into a long oval. Insert a marzipan oval into each date and press the sides of the dates lightly together.

★ Place the stuffed dates in petit-four cases and store in an airtight container in the refrigerator until about 30 minutes before they are required. Bring to room temperature before serving.

COOK'S NOTE
★ For more elaborate petits fours, cut open and stone the dates as described in the method. Wrap a blanched almond in a small piece of marzipan, shape into a roll with your fingers and insert into each date.

Christmas *Cake*

MAKES ONE 20-CM/8-INCH CAKE

150 g/5½ oz raisins
125 g/4½ oz stoned dried dates, chopped
125 g/4½ oz sultanas
100 g/3½ oz glacé cherries, rinsed
150 ml/5 fl oz brandy
225 g/8 oz butter, plus extra for greasing
200 g/7 oz caster sugar
4 eggs
grated rind of 1 orange
grated rind of 1 lemon
1 tbsp black treacle
225 g/8 oz plain flour
½ tsp salt
½ tsp baking powder
1 tsp mixed spice
25 g/1 oz toasted almonds, chopped
25 g/1 oz toasted hazelnuts, chopped
750 g/1 lb 10 oz marzipan
3 tbsp apricot jam, warmed
3 egg whites
650 g/1 lb 7 oz icing sugar
silver dragées and ribbon, to decorate

★ Make this cake at least 3 weeks in advance. Put all the fruit in a bowl and pour over the brandy. Cover and leave to soak overnight.

★ Preheat the oven to 110°C/225°F/Gas Mark ¼. Grease a 20-cm/8-inch cake tin with butter and line it with greaseproof paper. Cream the remaining butter and the sugar in a bowl until fluffy. Gradually beat in the eggs. Stir in the citrus rind and treacle. Sift the flour, salt, baking powder and mixed spice into a separate bowl, then fold into the egg mixture. Fold in the soaked fruit and brandy and the nuts, then spoon the mixture into the cake tin.

★ Bake in the preheated oven for at least 3 hours. If it browns too quickly, cover with foil. The cake is cooked when a skewer inserted into the centre comes out clean. Remove from the oven and leave to cool on a wire rack. Store in an airtight container until required.

★ Roll out the marzipan and cut to shape to cover the top and sides of the cake. Brush the cake with the jam and press the marzipan on to the surface. Make the icing by placing the egg whites in a bowl and adding the icing sugar a little at a time, beating well until the icing is very thick and will stand up in peaks. Spread over the covered cake, using a fork to give texture. Decorate as you wish with silver dragées and ribbon.

COOK'S NOTE

★ While the cake is being stored prior to icing, you can pierce several holes in the top with a skewer and drizzle lightly with brandy, sherry, Madeira wine or maraschino liqueur once a week to add extra flavour and keep it moist.

Shortbread

Slices

MAKES 16

BISCUIT BASE
125 g/4½ oz salted butter,
  plus extra for greasing
50 g/1¾ oz unrefined caster sugar
175 g/6 oz plain flour

TOPPING
100 g/3½ oz unrefined
  caster sugar
115 g/4 oz salted butter
200 g/7 oz condensed milk
2 tbsp golden syrup
200 g/7 oz mixed dried fruit
100 g/3½ oz mixed chopped nuts
200 g/7 oz milk chocolate,
  broken into pieces

★ Preheat the oven to 160°C/325°F/Gas Mark 3. Grease a 23-cm/9-inch square cake tin with butter and line it with greaseproof paper.

★ Dice the remaining butter, then place in a bowl with the sugar and flour and rub together to form a crumbly dough. Press firmly and evenly into the prepared cake tin and bake in the preheated oven for 30-35 minutes until golden. Leave to cool in the tin.

★ To make the toffee for the topping, melt the sugar and 100 g/3½ oz of the butter together slowly in a saucepan, then leave to simmer for 10 minutes until thick. Add the condensed milk and syrup and bring gently to the boil, stirring constantly. Reduce the heat and cook the toffee, scraping down the sides of the saucepan, for 5-10 minutes until the mixture is golden and thick – be careful not to overcook it. Pour over the biscuit base. Scatter over the fruit and nuts and press gently into the toffee. Leave to set in the refrigerator for 20 minutes.

★ Meanwhile, put the chocolate and the remaining butter in a heatproof bowl, set over a saucepan of barely simmering water and heat until melted and smooth. Spread the chocolate mixture over the set toffee and chill in the refrigerator for 2 hours. Cut the shortbread into 16 squares with a hot knife.

COOK'S NOTE
★ Instead of adding the fruit and nut layer, you can decorate the top with chopped glacé cherries or chopped nuts, drizzled white chocolate or chocolate-covered nuts.

Christmas Tree
Cookies

MAKES 12

150 g/5½ oz plain flour, plus extra
    for dusting
1 tsp ground cinnamon
½ tsp ground nutmeg
½ tsp ground ginger
70 g/2½ oz unsalted butter, diced,
    plus extra for greasing
3 tbsp honey

TO DECORATE
white icing (optional)
narrow gold or silver ribbon

★ Sift the flour and spices into a bowl and rub in the butter until the mixture resembles breadcrumbs. Add the honey and mix together well to form a soft dough. Wrap the dough in clingfilm and chill in the refrigerator for 30 minutes.

★ Meanwhile, preheat the oven to 180°C/350°F/Gas Mark 4 and lightly grease 2 baking sheets with butter. Divide the dough in half. Roll out 1 piece of dough on a floured work surface to about 5 mm/¼ inch thick. Cut out tree shapes using a cutter or cardboard template. Repeat with the remaining piece of dough.

★ Put the biscuits on the prepared baking sheets and, using a cocktail stick, make a hole through the top of each biscuit large enough to thread the ribbon through. Chill in the refrigerator for 15 minutes.

★ Bake the biscuits in the preheated oven for 10–12 minutes until golden. Leave to cool on the baking sheets for 5 minutes, then transfer to a wire rack to cool completely. Decorate the trees with white icing, or simply leave them plain, then thread a length of ribbon through each hole and knot. Hang from the Christmas tree.

COOK'S NOTE

★ Ice these biscuits with a mixture of coloured icing and silver dragées, and hang on the tree with matching ribbon, or put into cellophane bags and tie with a matching ribbon to give to friends.

Christmas Card

Tree Decoration

Would you like to give something a little more than a card, but you are not sure of what to buy? This clever card design doubles up as a stylish tree decoration.

MATERIALS

- ✳ 300 gsm brown card
- ✳ pale-green plain paper
- ✳ pale-green handmade-quality paper
- ✳ brown, red and gold glitter card
- ✳ brown corrugated card
- ✳ 8-cm/3¼-inch length of 5-mm/¼-inch wide dark-red ribbon
- ✳ 12-cm/4½-inch length of 2-mm/¹⁄₁₆-inch wide green ribbon
- ✳ deep-red glass bead, about 10-15 mm/½-⅝ inch in diameter
- ✳ small, double-backed self-adhesive pad
- ✳ pencil, craft knife, steel-edged ruler, cutting mat, bone folder or scoring tool, hole punch, glue stick, double-sided tape

✳ Enlarge the template on page 220 on a photocopier to the required size and cut out. Draw around the template on to the brown card and cut out with a craft knife and steel-edged ruler on a cutting mat. Score down the centre with a bone folder or scoring tool and fold. Punch a hole near the top.

✳ Cover the inside of the tree with glue stick. Stick the plain green paper on one half of the inside, placing it down the centre fold and making sure it adheres well. Trim with the craft knife. Repeat on the opposite side. Cut out the punched hole with the craft knife.

✳ Cut a trunk from brown glitter card and attach in two pieces to the front and back of the card with double-sided tape. Cut the container from brown corrugated card and attach in the same way.

✳ Attach the red ribbon with double-sided tape, running it over the card spine.

✳ Use glue stick to adhere the green handmade-quality paper in one piece to the front and back of the outside of the card. Cut out the punched hole.

✳ Create a loop for hanging from the green ribbon, threading the deep-red glass bead on to it before tying off. Attach the self-adhesive pad to the inside of the card for the recipient to use to fasten the card closed.

Christmas

Snowflake Cards

Just one template can be used to create four classy card designs that will look stunning on display in the home. You can, of course, use different coloured papers and spray paints to create a colour scheme of your choice.

MATERIALS

* card 3 mm/⅛ inch thick
* 300 gsm Bockingford (slightly textured) paper
* 300 gsm white card
* silver and/or gold spray paint
* silver and/or gold card
* pencil, craft knife, steel-edged ruler, cutting mat, masking tape, bone folder, double-sided tape, old newspaper, face mask and protective gloves

Enlarge the template on page 220 on a photocopier as directed and cut out with scissors. Draw around the template on to the 3-mm/⅛-inch thick card and cut out with a craft knife and steel-edged ruler on a cutting mat.

Place the template on the Bockingford paper and secure with masking tape. Ensure there is enough space to create a 15-cm/6-inch square. Turn the paper over and rub firmly all over the template area with a bone folder to create an impression.

Remove the template. Ensure that the embossed snowflake is in the centre of the paper, then trim to 15 cm/6 inches square.

Cut a piece of white card 15 x 30 cm/6 x 12 inches. Score down the centre with a bone folder and fold in half. Use double-sided tape around the edges of the embossed snowflake panel to attach it to the card.

Repeat steps 2 to 4 to create a second card, but adhere the Bockingford paper to the opposite side of the white card to create a reversed impression.

To make a third card, place the template on the front of folded white card (see step 4). Protect your work surface with old newspaper. Wearing a face mask and protective gloves, spray silver and/or gold paint over the card. When dry, remove the template to reveal the snowflake.

To make a fourth card, cut a piece of silver or gold card 15 x 30 cm/6 x 12 inches. Score down the centre with a bone folder and fold in half. Respray the snowflake template so that it contrasts with the card, if needed, and attach it to the card front with double-sided tape.

Christmas Card
Snowmen

Bring a smile to someone's face with this fun, quirky snowman card, with its wonderful three-dimensional quality. The arms of the metal foil snowmen are flexible enough to bring gently forwards to create more shadow behind.

MATERIALS

* 300 gsm white card
* scrap card
* roll of pewter lightweight metal foil
* 90 gsm white paper
* thick tracing paper 11.5 cm/4³/₈ inches square
* 2 ready-made embossed snowflakes, about 4.5 cm/1³/₄ inches in diameter
* pencil, craft knife, steel-edged ruler, cutting mat, bone folder or scoring tool, permanent black marker pen, wool needle, hole punch, double-sided tape, superglue

★ Using a craft knife and a steel-edged ruler on a cutting mat, cut a piece of the white card 12.5 x 25 cm/4³/₄ x 10 inches. Score down the centre with a bone folder or a scoring tool and fold in half. Copy the template on page 221 on a photocopier and cut out. Draw around the template on to scrap card and cut out with a craft knife and steel-edged ruler on a cutting mat. Draw around the template three times on to the foil using the marker pen.

★ Cut the snowmen out with the craft knife, but slightly change each one to give them individual character. For example, make the first snowman's hat taller, the second one's body larger and the third one's face a different shape.

★ Cut a strip of pewter foil 7 mm x 11.5 cm/³/₈ x 4³/₈ inches. Dab it all over with the wool needle to create texture. Punch about 24 dots from the white paper.

★ Attach the pewter strip about 7 mm/¹/₄ inch from the bottom of the tracing paper with double-sided tape. Place double-sided tape on the reverse of the tracing paper and pewter strip, and attach to the folded card, positioning it centrally.

★ Carefully lift the tracing paper to attach the embossed snowflakes to the card with double-sided tape. Add a few paper dots, ensuring that there are two in either top corner. Place a droplet of superglue on each of these corner dots to fasten the tracing paper securely. Stick another two paper dots to the tracing paper to hide the glue marks.

★ Attach the snowmen at different angles with double-sided tape, ensuring that they are butted up against the pewter strip. Add the remaining paper dots around the snowmen.

Tree Table *Decoration*

Bring a touch of elegance to your festive table with this unusual tree centrepiece. It can be made bigger or smaller by varying the number of hoops.

MATERIALS

* craft wire – thick (2 mm/¹⁄₁₆ inch) and thin
* 6 cylindrical objects descending in diameter, such as: plant pot measuring 13 cm/5 inches in diameter, body of wine bottle, mug, body lotion bottle, correction fluid bottle, neck of wine bottle
* reel of silver thread
* 1-metre/39-inch strings of silver beads in 3 varieties
* tiny glass turquoise and cobalt blue beads
* blue sequins
* 3 cobalt-blue glass droplets
* 3 cobalt-blue plastic leaf beads
* 4 turquoise glass 'bunches of grapes' beads
* silver elastic
* blue and clear plastic gems
* clear glass star with a hole, 2.5 cm/1 inch in diameter
* long-nosed pliers, tape measure, superglue

To make 6 wire hoops, wrap a length of the thick wire around each cylindrical object in turn, allow some surplus, then cut with the pliers. Twist the ends together to make each hoop fit tightly around the object, then trim the protruding ends of the twisted wire.

To create the 'trunk', cut a length of thick wire equal to the total of the height of the tree, half the diameter of the base hoop and an extra 2 cm/³⁄₄ inch to allow enough wire to attach it to the base hoop. So, for a tree 30 cm/12 inches high and with 13-cm/5-inch base hoop, you would need to cut a 38.5-cm/15¹⁄₄-inch length of thick wire. Use the first 5-10 mm/¹⁄₄-¹⁄₂ inch of the wire to form a loop. With the wire upright above the centre of the base hoop, make a right-angled bend 30 cm/12 inches from the top loop. Twist the last 1.5 cm/⁵⁄₈ inch around the base hoop with the pliers.

Cut a piece of the thin wire equal in length to the diameter of the next-largest hoop, plus 4 cm/1¹⁄₂ inches to attach the hoop to the 'trunk'. At the halfway point along the wire, wrap it around the trunk 5 cm/2 inches from the base hoop. Twist

either end around opposite points on the hoop. Cut 4 pieces of the wire 8 cm/3¹⁄₄ inches long. With each length, twist 1.5 cm/⁵⁄₈ inch at either end around the base hoop and the one above it at evenly spaced intervals. Attach the remaining hoops in the same way. Use 3 pieces of wire 5 cm/2 inches long to attach the smallest hoop to the small top loop.

Secure the end of the silver thread to the base hoop with superglue, then weave it all over the tree and glue to the top of the tree. Repeat with the strings of silver beads. Thread blue beads and sequins on to the thin wire and twist around the tree, securing either end by twisting around the hoops. Hang the glass droplets and other decorative beads at intervals from little loops of wire. Thread some on to silver elastic, using knots to secure them in place at various points. Superglue the blue and clear plastic gems in place. Use the wire to attach the glass star to the tree top.

TIP

Ensure there are no potentially harmful wire ends protruding by bending them towards the trunk with pliers.

Festive *Mobile*

Welcome family and friends into your home in style this Christmas by hanging this richly coloured mobile in your hallway.

MATERIALS

- light-green, dark-green, cream, and dark-red felt
- large sewing needle and embroidery thread: dark-red, sage-green and cream
- wadding
- 4 fabric hearts, about 1.5 cm/⅝ inch wide
- 4 red or wooden buttons, about 2 cm/¾ inch in diameter
- brass bell, about 2 cm/¾ inch in diameter
- red and dark-green ribbon
- inner wooden ring of an embroidery hoop, 20 cm/8 inches in diameter
- natural string
- 8 red beads, about 5 mm/¼ inch in diameter
- reel of transparent elastic
- craft wire
- scissors, tailor's chalk, craft knife, cutting mat, fabric glue, double-sided tape, superglue, long-nosed pliers, clear nail varnish

★ Enlarge the templates on page 220 on a photocopier as directed and cut out with scissors. Use tailor's chalk and either scissors or a craft knife and a cutting mat to cut 2 of the following from felt: light-green bell; dark-green star; cream rocking horse and heart; red soldier.

★ Using the pattern on page 220, cross-stitch a heart in both cream hearts. Hand sew the hearts and the other pairs of shapes together with a blanket stitch (see page 185) - use dark-red thread for the cream shapes and the bell, cream for the star and sage-green for the soldier. Just before you finish stitching each shape, slightly stuff with wadding. Using fabric glue, stick the fabric hearts to the rocking horse and star on either side.

★ Cover one side of 2 buttons with red felt and 2 with green felt using double-sided tape. Using sage green thread, sew through each button once, tie a knot at the back and trim the thread. Using fabric glue, stick a red button on either side of the bell and a green button on either side of the soldier. Sew the brass bell to the felt bell.

★ Tightly wrap red and green ribbon around the wooden hoop and use double-sided tape and superglue to fasten and secure it. Repeat with the string, wrapping it close together in some parts and spaced out in others to reveal the ribbon.

★ Cut different lengths of string for all the shapes except the heart, ranging from 45 cm/17¾ inches for the rocking horse to 5 cm/2 inches for the bell. Thread beads on to the strings and secure with knots at various points. Loop each string over the ring and superglue both ends to the top of each shape, positioning as shown.

★ Attach 4 evenly spaced lengths of transparent elastic to the ring, then join together on to a wire loop, formed with pliers, which can be used to attach the mobile to the ceiling. Sew a 25-cm/10-inch length of elastic to the centre top of the heart, then tie the other end to the metal loop and seal with clear nail vanish.

Snowflake *Gift Box*

This unusually shaped gift box is as practical as it is attractive. After you have made the printed fabric, you can use the silver snowflakes to make pretty confetti for the table.

MATERIALS

* sheet of paper
* old newspaper
* calico fabric 50 cm/ 20 inches square
* silver spray paint
* scrap card
* card 2 mm/¹⁄₁₆ inch thick
* matt silver paper
* felt-backed paper – black, silver, cream or light-blue
* tissue paper
* 300 gsm white card
* silver elastic
* craft knife, cutting mat, face mask and protective gloves, spray glue, hairspray, steel-edged ruler, gel superglue, strong self-adhesive binding tape, strong double-sided tape

✳ Enlarge the snowflake template on page 220 on a photocopier at various sizes – no set size is required, but you should be able to fit the largest snowflake on to one side of the box. Using scissors, cut around the outlines and attach to fill a sheet of paper. Photocopy the sheet 3 times. Cut out each snowflake with a craft knife on a cutting mat.

✳ Lay the newspaper down in a well-ventilated area, then lay the calico on top, ensuring that it is not creased. Wearing a face mask and protective gloves, spray the snowflakes with glue and scatter on to the calico, pressing down firmly around the edges. Spray the snowflakes and calico with silver paint. Leave to dry. Remove the silver snowflakes, then spray the calico lightly with hairspray to seal.

✳ Enlarge the box templates on page 221 on a photocopier as directed and cut out with scissors. Draw around the templates on to scrap card and cut out with a craft knife and steel-edged ruler on a cutting mat.

✳ Using the templates, cut all the pieces for the box out of the 2-mm/¹⁄₁₆-inch thick card. Place the base on newspaper and run gel superglue along one longer edge. Hold one of the sides vertically butted up against the base until completely dry and rigid. Repeal for the opposite side. Add the ends to the base and sides in the same way. Add the lid, using strong self-adhesive binding tape on the outside and inside, ensuring there is a gap of about 2 mm/¹⁄₁₆ inch (where the binding tape on the front and back will touch) to allow a good hinge.

✳ Starting with the lid, coat each box side with double-sided tape, including the edges. Adhere to the reverse of the calico and trim with the craft knife. Ensure that you leave enough fabric to wrap over the edges for a good finish. Line the inside with silver paper and the bottom with felt-backed paper. Add tissue paper.

✳ Cut a gift-tag shape from the white card, cover with offcuts of the calico using double-sided tape and thread with silver elastic. The elastic can be tied in a loop and stretched over the box to close it.

Gift *Tags*

A gift tag makes the perfect embellishment to a beautifully wrapped present, and here are a few ideas for making your own. These tags can also be made larger as greeting cards.

MATERIALS

HOLLY AND HEART TAGS

* 300 gsm white, green or red card
* red and sage-green felt
* sewing needle and deep-red embroidery thread
* holly leaf
* deep-red raw-silk fabric scraps
* red ribbon

PERSONALIZED PHOTO TAG

* 300 gsm white or red card
* gold or silver acrylic paint/ink
* family photograph
* red felt-tip pen
* correction fluid
* fine black pen
* pencil, craft knife, steel-edged ruler, cutting mat, hole punch, strong double-sided tape, old newspaper, paintbrush, bone folder

HOLLY AND HEART TAGS

★ Choose any colour card to make your gift tag to the size you require. Cut out a rectangular shape with a craft knife and steel-edged ruler on a cutting mat. Punch a hole in the corner.

★ Attach the red felt to the holly tag and the green felt to the heart tag with double-sided tape. Trim with the craft knife.

★ Using the sewing needle and embroidery thread, sew the holly leaf to the felt side of the tag with one cross-stitch (see page 185), tying the thread at the back and trimming the excess.

★ Cut 3 small squares of the silk and, using double-sided tape, adhere to the felt side of the heart tag, overlapping them at jaunty angles. Add a small sage green felt heart to one of the silk squares with double-sided tape.

★ Carefully cut the punched holes in the tags with the craft knife, thread a length of red ribbon through the each hole and make a knot in the ribbon.

PERSONALIZED PHOTO TAG

★ For the photo tag, enlarge the template on page 221 as directed and cut out with scissors. Transfer to the white or red card. Cut out, using a craft knife and a cutting mat, including the square window in the centre, but leave the white areas inside the bow (you can also cut them out).

★ Protect your work surface with old newspaper. Paint the light grey areas on the template with gold or silver paint, or ink, to complete the frame.

★ Take a black and white photocopy of the photograph, or print out a black-and-white copy, to fit the size of the tag window. Duplicate the image as many times as required. Add Father Christmas hats with red felt-tip pen and bobbles with correction fluid. When dry, outline the hats with a fine black pen. Cut the image out, leaving a border (especially at the top) to adhere it to the frame with double-sided tape. Adhere a folded card to the back of the tag for writing a message. Attach the tag to your gift with double-sided tape.

Country-style *Garland*

Perfect for creating a country cottage feel, this New England-style garland will bring warmth and traditional festive cheer to your home. Choose to make several short ones or a few longer ones to fit any size of wall, mantelpiece or stairwell.

MATERIALS

* small-weave hessian fabric 30 cm/12 inches square
* large-weave hessian fabric 30 cm/12 inches square
* scraps of pale-green and deep-red felt
* scraps of deep-red gingham and plain red cotton fabric
* natural string
* decorative gold fine thread or ribbon
* 5 red buttons, 2 cm/³⁄₄ inch in diameter
* embroidery needle and deep-red embroidery thread
* thin craft wire
* 6 tiny wooden pegs
* 2 tiny felt hearts
* scissors, tailor's chalk, craft knife, cutting mat, tape measure, fabric glue, long-nosed pliers, strong double-sided tape

⭐ Enlarge the templates on page 218 on a photocopier as directed and cut out using scissors. Using tailor's chalk and either scissors or a craft knife on a cutting mat, cut out the following: 2 circles from small-weave hessian, 2 from large-weave hessian; 2 large stars from each hessian, 1 small star from green felt; 4 angel bodies from large-weave hessian; 4 angel wings from small-weave hessian; 2 large hearts from red gingham, 2 from plain red; 2 small hearts from red gingham, 2 from plain red, 2 from green felt.

⭐ Lay a 1.5 m/59-inch length of string on a work surface and twist the gold thread around. Tie a loop at either end and fray the ends.

⭐ Cover one side of the buttons with fabric glue and adhere the red felt. Cut around the buttons with a craft knife. Pass the needle and thread through the buttonholes once so the thread ends dangle from the back of the button by about 1.5 cm/⁵⁄₈ inch. Ensure 2 of the buttons have extra thread hanging.

✦ Arrange the embellishments above the string, working out from the centre. Run a length of thin wire around the top of the red and gingham large hearts with pliers and use double-sided tape to sandwich between the fabrics. Glue a small green heart to the plain red side and add one of the buttons. Use 2 pegs to attach to the string.

✦ Construct the angels in the same way, but simply sandwich the string in between the head and tops of the wings. Sandwich the wings (2 sets per angel) in between the bodies. Glue the tiny felt hearts in place.

✦ Construct the remaining embellishments in the same way, using wire to strengthen them, and attach to the string.

Christmas Door
Wreath

This simple but effective door decoration will be admired by all who visit, yet it doesn't demand any sophisticated floristry skills. For an alternative look, experiment with various fabric combinations, ribbons and string, and use other embellishments in place of the holly, bearing in mind that it needs to withstand the weather conditions if not sheltered.

MATERIALS

* plain deep-red fabric, red gingham and ruby raw-silk fabric, each 2.5 cm x 1.5 metres/ 1 inch x 59 inches
* polystyrene wreath 24 cm/9½ inches in diameter
* red gingham 2.5 cm x 50 cm/1 x 20 inches
* 21 holly leaves, 16 about 6 cm/2½ inches in length and 5 about 4 cm/1½ inches in length
* floristry wire
* 2 fir cones on wire about 5 cm/2 inches in length
* fake berries on flexible stems
* tape measure, scissors, strong double-sided tape, long-nosed pliers

Wrap the red fabric strip around the wreath – the point at which you start and finish will become the bottom of the wreath. Use double-sided tape to secure the ends. Do not worry about covering all the polystyrene at this stage.

Repeat with the larger length of gingham, starting and ending in the same place and focusing on covering more of the polystyrene. Repeat with the raw silk to cover the remaining polystyrene.

Wrap the smaller piece of gingham over where the other strips started and ended as many times as possible, tying the ends in a tight knot. Trim the ends. Use the scissors to trim any stray threads.

Thread all the holly leaves with the floristry wire, using the pliers to help direct the wire into the main veins of the holly. The smaller leaves should be together. Use the pliers to pierce all around the polystyrene wreath and insert the large holly leaves into the holes. The smaller leaves should be by the wrapped gingham.

Gently push the fir cones under the wrapped gingham with the berries, and finish with the smaller wired holly in between. Push a length of wire into the back of the wreath to make a loop to hang the wreath.

Festive *Frame*

Frame your family members in festive spirit. If you have the time, make one for each family member in a different size for a special collection.

MATERIALS

* image transfer paste
* colour photocopy or printout of family photograph
* calico fabric 18 cm/ 7 inches square
* 300 gsm white card
* foam board, 5 mm/¼ inch thick, measuring 25.5 x 31 cm/10¼ x 12½ inches
* deep-red cotton fabric 50 cm/20 inches square
* 5-mm/¼-inch thick board 30 cm/12 inches square
* ruby-red raw-silk 15 x 30 cm/6 x 12 inches
* 20-cm/8-inch length of 7-mm/¼-inch wide ruby-red ribbon
* 30-cm/12-inch length of 3-mm/⅛-inch wide green ribbon
* 6 holly leaves, about 4 cm/1½ inches in length
* wired fake red berries
* 300 gsm deep-red card
* metal picture hook
* sponge, paintbrush, kitchen paper, rolling pin, craft knife, steel-edged ruler, cutting mat, strong double-sided tape, superglue

Using the image transfer paste, transfer your image on to the calico fabric. When dry, back it with the white card using double-sided tape, ensuring that the fabric is taut.

Cut a square of foam board large enough to frame your image. Cut an aperture in the board to give your image a 2-cm/¾-inch wide calico borde.

Stick double-sided tape around the edges of the foam board frame on both sides. Adhere the red cotton fabric tightly to the frame front. Cut 2 diagonal lines joining the two sets of opposing inner corners of the frame. Fold the triangles back, pull tightly and adhere to the frame back. Trim the excess. At each corner, make two cuts from the outer edges of the fabric to form a right angle and cut away the fabric corners. Fold the fabric neatly over the frame, pull tightly and adhere to the frame. Trim the excess. Use scraps of fabric to cover up any exposed foam.

Place the thick board square on the silk fabric and cut around it with a craft knife on a cutting mat. Cut as many squares as you need to cover just under half the height of the frame. Attach double-sided tape to the squares to prevent fraying. Attach to the frame, alternating the weave from horizontal to vertical, folding the fabric over the sides. At the frame corners, snip the fabric diagonally into the corner and fold over the frame.

Place double-sided tape on to the red ribbon and use to trim the top of the silk squares. Repeat with the green ribbon, about 1 cm/½ inch from the top. Use double-sided tape to secure the ends to the back.

'Hang' the holly leaves from the green ribbon with double-sided tape, three either side of the wired fake berries, which are hooked over the top edge of the frame.

Place double-sided tape on the four corners of the calico border and attach to the back of the frame, ensuring the image faces outwards from the aperture.

Cut a piece of the red card 2 cm/¾ inch less in length and width than the frame. Use to back the frame, securing it with double-sided tape. Glue a picture hook to the centre back, about 6 cm/2½ inches from the top.

Festive *Napkin Holders*

These decorative napkin holders can be tailored to your colour theme by selecting ribbons and beads to coordinate. Try different beads, such as those with letters for a personal touch.

MATERIALS

* craft wire – thick (2 mm/¹⁄₁₆ inch) and thin
* ready-made solid napkin ring
* beige thick cotton fabric
* sewing needle and beige strong cotton thread
* beads of your choice
* ribbons to match or coordinate with the beads and fabric
* white Velcro™
* scissors, long-nosed pliers, tape measure, tailor's chalk, strong double-sided tape, extra-strong iron-on hemming tape, steam iron

✴ Lay the thick craft wire across the width of the napkin ring, then bend it at a right angle around the ring until it is about 3.5 cm/1³⁄₈ inches away from the right-angled bend. Bend the wire at a right angle across the ring, then again at a right angle round the other side of the ring in the other direction until you reach the beginning of the wire. Cut the wire, leaving enough surplus to twist the ends together with the pliers. Repeat for the number of napkin holders you require.

✴ Measure the width and length of one of the napkin holders and add 1.5 cm/⁵⁄₈ inch to each measurement. Cut two pieces of beige fabric this size for each napkin holder. On one of each pair of fabric pieces, use tailor's chalk to mark the measurements of the napkin holder, centred. Pierce through the fabric at each corner with a needle so that you can see its position on the other side.

✴ On the needle-pricked side of the fabric, place double-sided tape along both lengths and widths, flush to the edges. Trim the corners for a neat finish. Align a napkin holder with the pricked holes at one end. Remove the tape backing and fold the fabric edges over the wire to secure. You can sew along all the edges for extra security.

✴ Using the iron-on hemming tape and following the manufacturer's instructions, hem the edges of the second piece of fabric so that it is 5 mm/¹⁄₄ inch smaller all round than the napkin holder.

✴ Thread your chosen beads on to a length of the thin wire, then wrap around the napkin holder. Pierce the ends through the fabric and fold over firmly to ensure that the beads are held securely and the wire doesn't protrude. Wrap the ribbon around, securing it at the back with double-sided tape for easy removal.

✴ Back the napkin holder with the second hemmed piece of fabric, using thin strips of Velcro™ for easy removal.

TIP

✴ Alternatively, you can sew the beads and ribbon on to the napkin holder fabric for a permanent result. Sponge clean the fabric only.

Reindeer Tea-light *Box*

This reindeer-adorned light box, illuminated by the soft glow of tea lights, will add atmosphere to any area of your home. Try the mantelpiece, dining table or a stairwell.

MATERIALS

* 300 gsm Bockingford (slightly textured) paper
* thick tracing paper
* board 2 mm/1/16 inch thick
* clear glass tea-light holders
* tea lights
* scissors, masking tape, craft knife, steel-edged ruler, cutting mat, bone folder or scoring tool, strong double-sided tape

Enlarge the box templates on page 219 on a photocopier as directed and cut out using scissors. You may need to make the template in two halves.

Place the light box template over the Bockingford paper on a cutting mat and secure both with masking tape. Using the craft knife, cut out as many of the reindeer shapes as you want, depending on how many sides will be visible.

Cut out the light box, marking the position of the folds by piercing through to the paper at each end of the fold lines as you cut around. Remove the template. Align the ruler with the puncture marks and score along the lines with a bone folder or scoring tool.

Cut the tracing paper to the size of the panels from which you have cut motifs. Secure to the panels with double-sided tape along the top and bottom edges.

Construct the box, using double-sided tape to adhere the hem inside at the top of the box, for extra rigidity, and the side seam. Fold up the bottom of the box – it should look like the back of an envelope – using a few strips of double-sided tape in different directions to secure it.

Using the rectangular template, cut the platform from the board, then slot into the base of the light box. Place the tea lights in clear glass tea-light holders no less than 6 cm/2½ inches high and position centrally within the box. Use no more than 2 tea lights per box.

WARNINGS

Never leave lit candles unattended.

Do not make this light box smaller than instructed.

Do not place tea lights inside the light box without glass holders.

Do not lift the box when the tea lights are lit without supporting it underneath.

Advent *Calendar*

Every child knows that when the Advent calendar is hung, Christmas isn't too far away. Build the excitement by choosing your own treats and sentiments to fill this delightful calendar.

MATERIALS

* beige thick cotton fabric 1 metre/39 inches square
* red and dark-green felt
* roll of matt laminate
* 2 pieces of bamboo cane 36 cm/14¼ inches in length
* bright-red soft thick fabric 62 x 93 cm/25 x 37 inches
* sewing needle and deep-red strong cotton thread
* extra-strong iron-on hemming tape
* 6 pairs of deep-red baby socks, age 0–3 months
* 6 pairs of deep-green baby socks, age 0–3 months
* 25 Christmas-tree embellishments in red, green and gold
* 24 tiny wooden pegs
* 1.5-metres/59 inches of 1-cm/½-inch wide green ribbon
* large silver bell
* 36-cm/14¼-inch length of 5-mm/¼-inch wide red ribbon
* craft knife, steel-edged ruler, pinking shears, tacking pins, tacking thread, strong double-sided tape, scissors, steam iron, fabric glue

⭐ Enlarge the box templates on page 219 on a photocopier as directed and cut out using scissors. Cut 24 squares from the beige fabric using a craft knife and a steel-edged ruler on a cutting mat. Cut 24 squares from red felt with pinking shears.

⭐ Using the template, cut the tree from green felt, place on the beige fabric and cut out a slightly larger tree for a border.

⭐ Laminate the sheet of numbers, then cut out with the craft knife and ruler.

⭐ Place one length of bamboo at the top of the large piece of red fabric and fold the top edge of the fabric over. Pin, then tack the hem. Hand sew with red thread, then remove the tacking stitches. Repeat at the bottom of the fabric.

⭐ Temporarily position all the beige squares and the beige tree on the red fabric with double-sided tape, ensuring that they are evenly positioned. Using the iron-on hemming tape around the edges and following the manufacturer's instructions, adhere them to the red fabric one row at a time.

⭐ Using fabric glue, adhere the red felt squares about halfway up and 5 mm/¼ inch in from the right-hand side. Use double-sided tape to adhere the numbers centrally to each red square. Adhere the green felt tree to the beige tree with fabric glue. Sew the socks to the top corners of the beige squares. Open them fully to add your treats, then stick the heels down with fabric glue. Use fabric glue to adhere the tree embellishments, ensuring sock number 24 has 2 slightly overlapping trees. Add the pegs to look like they are holding the socks up. Tie bows in the green ribbon, attach the bell and sew to the tree in the bottom right-hand corner.

⭐ To create hanging loops, use the craft knife to make horizontal incisions just below the bamboo, wide enough to thread the red ribbon through and under the bamboo. Slightly overlap the ribbon and sew together. Move the ribbon around to hide the sewn part behind the bamboo. Repeat at the opposite end.

Star Tree *Topper*

Create this stunning tree topper and watch it shimmer as the light catches it at various angles. You could make matching 'baubles' by simply reducing the size, eliminating the spiral and adding a loop for hanging.

MATERIALS

- ✳ craft wire – thick (about 2 mm/¹⁄₁₆ inch) and thin
- ✳ silver thin shimmering thread
- ✳ silver beads and cotton thread
- ✳ 5 glass crystal beads
- ✳ scissors, craft knife, cutting mat, long-nosed pliers, gel superglue

✳ Enlarge the template on page 221 on a photocopier as directed and cut out with scissors.

✳ Using the pliers, bend a length of the thick wire into the star template shape, starting from the centre at the bottom.

✳ When you reach your starting point, bend the metal vertically down from the base of the star and begin to create a spiral about 6 cm (2½ inches) in length with 7 coils, making it wider at the bottom (about 5 cm/2 inches in diameter) – this is where the top of the tree will feed through it to secure the star. These measurements are only an approximate guide.

✳ Close the gap between where you began the star and where the wire was bent vertically down by slightly overlapping the wire and criss-crossing the thin wire around the wire to bind.

✳ Tie the silver thread securely to this point and weave it around the star to create a web. Thread silver beads on to the cotton thread (about 50 cm/20 inches in length) and coil around the stem and up on to the web, forming a squiggle by gently weaving in and out. Secure in place with tiny droplets of gel superglue.

✳ Thread each crystal bead on to a small loop of wire to attach to the five points of the star.

TIP

✳ Thread some extra crystal beads on to thin wire and weave around the top of the tree and the spiral to enhance the effect.

Templates

Country-style
Garland (enlarge by 200%)

Angel Card Tree Decoration
(enlarge by 200%)

Advent Calendar
(enlarge by 200%)

1	2	3	4
5	6	7	8
9	10	11	12
13	14	15	16
17	18	19	20
21	22	23	24

Reindeer Tea-light Box (enlarge by 400%)

Festive Mobile (enlarge by 200%, cross stitch pattern for visual reference only)

Christmas Snowflake Card
and Snowflake Gift Box
(enlarge by 200%)

Christmas Card Tree Decoration
(enlarge by 200%)

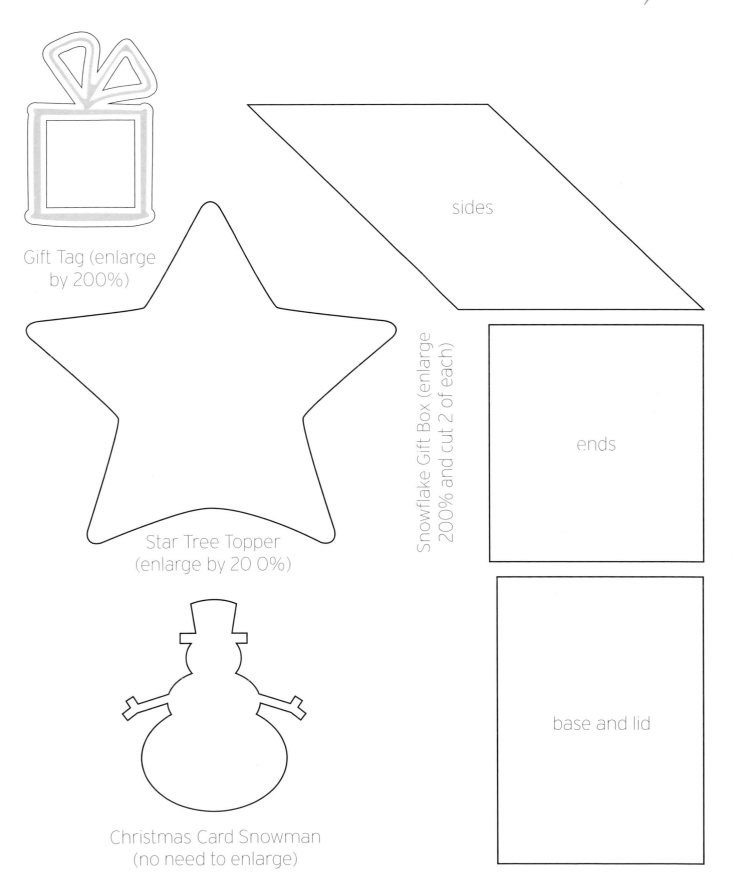

Gift Tag (enlarge
by 200%)

Star Tree Topper
(enlarge by 20 0%)

Snowflake Gift Box (enlarge
200% and cut 2 of each)

sides

ends

base and lid

Christmas Card Snowman
(no need to enlarge)